Fabricating Origins

Working with Culture on the Edge
Edited by Vaia Touna, University of Alberta

This series of small books draws on revised versions of posts that originally appeared online at edge.ua.edu – the blog for Culture on the Edge, a research collaborative engaged in rethinking identity studies. Each chapter is complemented by an original response from an early career scholar outside the group, that presses the chapter in new directions, either by applying its approach to novel situations or by offering a critique that enhances the approach. Each volume in the series therefore demonstrates how to work with a more dynamic, historically-sensitive approach to identity, as exemplified at a host of ordinary social sites – on varied themes, from museums and popular music to ordering at fast-food restaurants. The brief chapters retain the informality of blogging, modeling for readers how scholars can better examine the contingent and therefore changeable practices that help to create the conditions in which we claim to be an enduring something.

Each volume opens with a brief general Introduction to the key word on which it focuses and ends with an annotated list of Suggested Readings. The Afterword tackles wider issues of relevance to the volume's main theme.

Ideal for a variety of classes in which identity or the past are discussed, these small books can either set the table for more in-depth readings in a course or be paired with their suggested resources to comprise an entire course's readings. Thoroughly collaborative, cross-disciplinary, and cross-generational in nature, *Working with Culture on the Edge* provides an opportunity to rethink identity with a group of scholars committed to pressing identity studies in new directions.

Fabricating Origins

Edited by
Russell T. McCutcheon

SHEFFIELD UK BRISTOL CT

Published by Equinox Publishing Ltd.
UK: Office 415, The Workstation, 15 Paternoster Row, Sheffield,
       South Yorkshire S1 2BX
USA: ISD, 70 Enterprise Drive, Bristol, CT 06010

www.equinoxpub.com

First published 2015

British Library Cataloguing-in-Publication Data
A catalogue record for this book is available from the British Library.

ISBN-13 978 1 78179 174 5 (hardback)
         978 1 78179 175 2 (paperback)

Library of Congress Cataloging-in-Publication Data
Fabricating origins / edited by Russell T. McCutcheon.
  pages cm. – (Working with culture on the edge)
Includes bibliographical references and index.
ISBN 978-1-78179-174-5 (hb) – ISBN 978-1-78179-175-2 (pb)
1. Events (Philosophy) 2. Identity (Psychology) 3. Autobiographical
memory–Philosophy. 4. Explanation. 5. Culture on the edge (Research
group)–Blogs. I. McCutcheon, Russell T., 1961- editor. II. Culture on the
edge (Research group)
B105.E7F33 2015
901–dc23
                          2014044379

Typeset by S.J.I. Services, New Delhi
Printed and bound in Great Britain by Lightning Source UK Ltd., Milton Keynes
and Lightning Source Inc., La Vergne, TN

Contents

"Winter used to be so much colder; why, I remember the snow being over my knees when I was a kid."

"Yes…, but your knees were a lot closer to the ground back then."
– My father's reply to a friend's comment

Preface

Culture on the Edge grew out of a collaborative experience that Steven Ramey, Merinda Simmons, and I had, back in the Spring of 2011, at the University of Alabama, in which we worked together on a common project (in that case it was helping our College of Arts & Sciences to plan a semester's worth of activities related to what was then the early stages of our still ongoing Alabama/Greece Initiative). Given how much we enjoyed working together, a little brainstorming when that was over led to our discovery of a shared frustration with the way in which scholars who think they're developing new and provocative approaches to the study of how identities develop and blend (e.g., diaspora studies along with hybridization and creolization studies) are, in fact, often falling back on some traditional, and theoretically problematic, assumptions about how it is that we each come to feel ourselves to be members of groups. Voila – the birth of a new project to work on together. A little additional brainstorming and we came up with the names of a few others who we thought also shared this frustration and who might be up for inventing a new social group of our own – Craig Martin, Monica R. Miller, Leslie Dorrough Smith, and Vaia Touna. What then formed was an online and in-person collaborative research group that, we all hoped, would produce publications that pressed readers, in a variety of academic fields, to consider studying not identity itself but, instead, the discourse on identity – that is, acts and claims of identification that allow people to constitute the experience of being a this as opposed to a that.

Among the projects the group tackled was a scholarly blog – edge.ua.edu – written for a wide readership but always trying to press the envelope just a little, by inviting readers not merely to examine the products of social life but, instead, the procedures that led to just certain things eventually attracting our attention as legitimate and enduring. For instance, instead of studying values, let's examine the practical conditions that led to this specific set of interests standing out as the one worth pursuing, advocating, or maybe even fighting for. After a while, it became apparent that certain common themes were continually arising in our posts, one of which was the way that discourses on origins (much like the tale I'm spinning in this very preface, perhaps?) are continually drawn upon by social actors in a strategically useful way to authorize or contest something in the present – that is, like good lawyers in a court, we never cite a precedent that undermines our current interests, suggesting that the selection of just what to count as an origin, an authoritative starting point (like my mention of our working together on that Alabama/Greece Initiative), was always determined by particular choosers, in the present (in this case, me, the author of this text), the ones who have a specific goal in mind, a specific present they wish to work toward in their developmental narrative. After all, to the simple question "Where are you from?" we each have an exponentially increasing number of possible answers with every generation we go back. So, the question is: which family line – initially, is it your mother's or your father's, the matrilineal or the patrilineal? – do you choose, in tracing your origins back either to this celebrated monarch or that banished criminal? Our hunch is that the choice is not random – we need to know whether we wish to spin a tale of noble birth or one of triumphant rise from ignoble ashes, before we can decide which line gets to stand out and which is to be ignored.

Realizing that this approach to origins – as a product of prior sets of interests that are always in the present – unified a variety of posts on our blog, and knowing that publishing our work was a goal, prompted the group to propose a new book series that would make use of these blog posts, lightly revised, retaining their succinct and easily read style. The blogs would invite a brand new group of early career scholars to work with the material, to produce not just replies or commentaries but original essays that, though equally pithy, would pack a theoretical punch of their own, pressing the original pieces, critiquing them if necessary, or exemplifying the approach at a new site, thereby modeling for the reader yet again how to make the shift from talking about origins to problematizing how and why it is that we all seem to talk about origins as if they are pristine, free-floating moments in the past (big bangs, if you will), from which the present inevitably flows.

And that's how this new book series with Equinox Publishers, edited by Vaia Touna, of which *Fabricating Origins* is the first volume, arose. All of the volumes in the *Working with Culture on the Edge* series will retain much the same organization and rationale – modeling a shift in focus for readers and doing so by pairing early career scholars (perhaps working on their own PhD at the time when they wrote their chapter) with members of our research group. That we're all scholars of religion, though writing on culture-wide activities for readers in a variety of academic disciplines, hopefully says something not about how special our objects of study are but, instead, how useful the tools are that we employ to make sense of the things that happen to interest us. Our hope is also that the model we've adopted to do our work and to produce this volume sends a strong message not just on the importance (even the inevitability) of collaboration but on the role of collaboration across the various stages into which we commonly divide the career of being a scholar. It is worth observing, then, that, at the time of writing the chapters of this book, eleven of the contributors did not have the PhD degree, another four were tenure-track Assistant Professors, and only two others were tenured. And, with this variety of career stages in mind, the books are aimed at novice but motivated readers – whether undergraduate students or more seasoned scholars new to, but game to, making the shift that we're pursuing here at Culture on the Edge: the move away from merely describing identity to studying its creation, the "operational acts of identification" (as phrased by Jean-François Bayart in a book of importance to our group, *The Illusion of Cultural Identity* [2005]). With this broad range of readership in mind, we've intentionally retained the tactical feel of the blogging genre – there's always more to read if the volume's approach hooks you, and that's why we've included a list of suggested readings and films, to which all the authors in the volume have contributed, all of which are annotated so that readers understand why we think that each particular work might be relevant for helping them to rethink the socio-political role played by origins tales. And, of course, an introduction and a substantive afterword press further our collective analysis of the conditions and functions of this thing we're calling the discourse on origins.

Easily read and useful in a variety of class settings, we're hoping that *Working With Culture on the Edge* will make a timely contribution to promoting more than just descriptions and repetitions of what people are already saying about their own lives and who they are, and encourage the addition of a dose of social theory to how it is that we study who (and, perhaps more importantly, how) we all claim to be.

Introduction

Midnight in the Study of Origins

Russell T. McCutcheon

> Paul: You know…, nostalgia is denial. Denial of the painful present.
> Inez: Oh, whoa! Gil is a complete romantic. I mean, he would be more than happy living in a complete state of perpetual denial.
> Carol: Really?
> Paul: And the name for this fallacy is called "golden-age thinking."
> Inez: Ah, touché.
> Paul: Yeah, the erroneous notion that a different time period is better than the one one's living in. You know, it's a flaw in the Romantic imagination of those people who…, who find it difficult to cope with the present.
> – Woody Allen's *Midnight in Paris* (2011)

Among the assorted knick-knacks that line my office's shelves – ranging from such relics as photos of friends and family or gifts that I've accumulated over the years to a selection of tattered romance novels shelved among my books by mischievous students long ago – is a nicely matted and framed "fossil" of Knightia, a long-extinct genus of small, bony North American freshwater fish, dating to more than 35 million years ago (or what scientists call the Eocene epoch), and which was recovered from the well-known (to fossil hunters, at least) Green River Formation in southwestern Wyoming. I bought it, heavy wooden frame and all, one summer over ten years ago in a gift shop in downtown Iowa City, at the same time that I purchased for my Department's library a number of other artifacts, including a stereotypical dancing Shiva statue and a Thai-style bust of Buddha, complete with its intricately carved curls. I never anticipated writing about my framed piece of sedimentary rock that, for whatever reason, has found a home among the Ks in my shelving taxonomy (yes, I shelve books by author's surname), though I have often used it in classes to illustrate a point or two about discourses on origins; I now realize that this rock might have some use outside of the classroom.

That I have placed the word fossil in quotations marks the first time I use it, just above, signals what I do with it in classes: I use it to prompt students to consider where originality or antiquity resides – is it a quality that, akin to the formation of sedimentary rock, somehow accumulates within objects over time, layer by epochal layer, or is it a product of the habit of speech and the styles of behavior (in a word, discourses) that we employ, always in the present, to identify things *as* young or *as* old? I admit that as soon as one meets the empty stare of this bony little fish's burnt orange-colored skeleton, lying outstretched in two dimensions, having become virtually one with the yellowed rock, one can't help but *see it as* a fossil (unless you're among those, notably in the US, who consider evolutionary theory to be an ungodly hoax, then you see it in an entirely different manner, of course – nicely illustrating my point, perhaps?), and thus *as* something that is very, very, very old.

And so, when I put this on the seminar table and pose my inevitable question, "How old is that?" there routinely come immediate and confident replies from my students, spanning millions to tens of millions of years. But then I observe to them that this ancient object is actually in their own hands, at this very moment, making it necessarily contemporaneous with them – for if we can see it and feel it, then it is in the present and no matter how hard we stare at it (somewhat like an old-school literary critic giving a text a "close reading" so as to recover the long departed author's original meaning), we're not doing any time-traveling. So with this point established (whether or not I've *yet* convinced them...) we end up talking about not *how old it is* but, rather, *how we know that it is old*!

That it has yellowed is often a key marker. Sometimes I'll then talk about how, in grade school, we used to try and make our drawings "look" old by tearing the edges and crumpling them (because we all know that old things are in rough shape and wrinkled, right?) and then, with the help of our parents, either briefly soak them in tea or spread butter on them and then lightly bake them on low heat in the oven, like roasting cherry tomatoes, so that the paper would turn brown. The curious fact was, the new-looking paper that went into the tea or the oven would be older than the old-looking paper that came out minutes later. As children, we overlooked that, of course. But can we afford to overlook this point as scholars? Probably all this convinces no one of anything much in my classes, for our confidence in the depth of the past and our ability to plumb it, as careful historians, is pretty strong. But thinking for a moment about how it is that we know something to be old certainly makes students pause and think – and that's what this brief exercise is all about: practicing the sort of self-reflection that Jonathan Z. Smith once suggested was a scholar's "primary expertise" (1982: xi). And it usually works, for when I re-pose the question that the first time seemed so simple – "How old is that?" – students are not nearly so quick to answer. For they've shifted their attention from the self-evidently old thing to their possible role, as seemingly passive observers and historians, in actively producing the evidence itself: their presumptions about this foreign land called "the past" where origins are thought to reside.

So when I'm trying to complicate the way my students think about the past – about how they talk and write about it (what today goes by the name of doing history) and about the elusive noun to which that pronoun "it" refers – I will often bring out an object like that fossil, something that is pretty obviously old and put it in front of them and ask them to start talking about it. Most recently, I did this with a small, dark gray rock with white striations in it, that usually sits somewhere on a shelf with all the other objects in my cluttered office; it is sort of rectangular and it easily fits in the palm of your hand, and you can almost make a fist around it if you hold it tightly. I passed it around the class on the first day of a course dedicated to thinking through some issues that revolve around people talking about their tradition or heritage (asked why they do such-and-such, someone might reply, "Because, it's our tradition!" and that's really not an explanation so much as a recycling of the question: we do it because we do it; surely the academic study of tradition can do better than merely repeat this). As the rock went from student to student I asked them what it was. Now, students know something's up, of course, when asked a deceptively simple question like this, much as when a professor asks a leading question that signals that there's a right and a wrong answer; but being the first day of class, and not yet even knowing much about what our course was to achieve, they had little choice but to play along without any context that would guide them on how to answer my question. So I heard a lot of "it's a rock" or "it's a cold rock" as it made its way around the room – an upper-level undergraduate seminar with about sixteen students. Each of them held it briefly and took a stab at a description of this otherwise nondescript item – noteworthy to them merely because of the authority they granted me as their professor, and then my use of that authority to, let's be honest, force their attention toward a gray stone.

As that unremarkable object made its way back to me, I followed the last description with one of my own, stating: "This is a piece of Mount Olympus from Greece."

My description had the desired effect – a bit of a hush fell on the room, a couple of students then laughed uncertainly, and then they all turned toward the multimedia projection screen to see a large photo I had just displayed there. This was a shot of me at, yes, Mount Olympus, in the summer of 2011, accompanied by two other members of Culture on the Edge, Vaia Touna and Merinda Simmons (both of whom have chapters in this volume).

"What you just held in your hands is from one of the most famous mountains in the world," I continued, then adding "...or maybe it's just a rock."

My point?

From the outset of the course I was trying to interest the students in the term "discourse," whose scholarly use now includes a much more complicated concept than mere conversation. I was trying to insert a wedge, in a subtle but wily sort of way, into their taken-for-granted view of the world, so as to make some room, by means of that little rock they passed around, for a more critical approach to how it is that we talk about ourselves and who we think we are (or are not). And, mulling over how I wanted to start that first day of class, it occurred to me that, in a classroom in Alabama, it was likely that students knew their fair share about, say, ancient Greek mythology – whether in detail or not – yet probably none had ever traveled to Greece, let alone driven a tiny Greek car up the narrow, gravel roads on that mountain. So it seemed to me that the full meaning of "Greece" – going beyond the commonly held concepts of the place derived from anthologies of ancient narratives marketed to children, or the names given to frats and sororities on the university campus, and even the pomp and circumstance of the Olympic Games – might become evident to my students, in a way that it usually is not, in that moment when, because of my description, a mere rock suddenly was transformed into *a Greek rock* or, better put, an artifact from a mythical, maybe even sacred, mountain half a world away.

But then, to bring this illustration all the way back to the topic of the course, I asked them a question or two that made evident that the significance they now attributed to the rock was exactly that – *their attribution*, not the rock's intrinsic possession or property. Or, to put it another way, the rock hadn't changed at all; instead, they had changed by listening to my claim about traveling, picking up a rock, bringing it home, etc., then trusting my claim (I could have picked it up outside class, after all), and then forming a series of associations and conclusions of their own. They now saw that rock in a brand new light, one made possible by a discourse on Greece that, in my simple description of that rock, was suddenly placed upon it by all of us.

Introducing the role played by discourse – the complexly interwoven sets of assumptions, institutions, practices, and their practical effects – provided the opening for us to discuss what makes some objects, as I phrased it above, "pretty obviously old." Brittle to the touch? Yellowed? Said to be old by an authority figure? What's more, it allowed us to start a discussion on the difference between just old and significantly old. After all, virtually every rock you pick up is old, event ancient, inestimatably archaic in fact, if we are prepared (as not everyone is, of course) to talk about the past as geologists now do, as a length of time that stretches back millions of years. But although every rock might be equally ancient, not every rock is equally interesting. Or, to put it another way, just because something is old doesn't make it an antique, for many people's houses are filled with all sorts of old things they take for granted – "Oh, that old thing?" they might say. But, give it another setting and another set of interests – say, that of a far younger shopper browsing in an antique shop, intent on redecorating his/ her home in some retro style – and suddenly that plain old chair becomes a much coveted collector's item whose value would shock the person who once sat on it at a kitchen table playing cards or cleaning green beans so many years before.

Like the gray stone, the chair hasn't changed. But the set of interests that make the chair significant or not, valuable or not, certainly have. Somewhat like that yellowed rock from southwestern Wyoming, put into a nice frame by someone, it is now a fossil, an artifact.

And it was this shift – from seeing just any old thing to seeing how we signify just any old thing *as* something worth paying attention to, maybe even literally worth paying for – that I was hoping my Olympian rock could accomplish for the class. And it did; it prompted the students to start to pay a little more attention to themselves as the signifiers, to the criteria they employ to make items in the world interesting *to them*, worth talking about *for them*, worth preserving *by them* or, maybe, worth tossing away and forgetting altogether. It was a shift that made talking about the past as if it was a fixed, originary point in time, at a considerable distance from ourselves, a little more complicated than it previously had seemed, for now every rock was equally old; but *this* rock stood out nonetheless – though only if we came armed with a set of assumptions about what that faraway mountain meant to us. The meaning of the rock, the significance of the past, thus became ongoing works in the present, actions that made it meaningful, that made it significant, all taking place in the current moment in which generic objects and discourses meet.

I once used Woody Allen's recent film, *Midnight in Paris* (2011) – from which the epigraph to this introduction derives – in class to accomplish much the same thing. The main character, Gil, played by Owen Wilson – who Paul, his fiancée's pedantic and pompous friend (and, we learn later, lover), thinks is suffering from "golden-age thinking" – is a successful Hollywood screenwriter trying his hand at writing a novel, and not having much success. Visiting Paris with his less-than-supportive fiancée, Inez, and her equally less-than-supportive parents, he ends up strolling alone through what he (and not they) considers Paris's romantic streets, late at night. At the stroke of midnight one evening, a chauffeur-driven vintage (to Gil's eyes, at least) car pulls up, and he is somehow immediately transported back to Paris of the 1920s, meeting those now famous, and much idolized by him, ex-pat American writers, Fitzgerald, Hemingway, Stein, along with a host of other literary and artistic luminaries from that era – Picasso, Dali, Man Ray, etc. Each evening he finds an excuse to go for a stroll and each evening he joins his 1920s friends, attending their parties and getting feedback from them on his novel.

> Hemingway: You writing?
> Gil: A novel.
> Hemingway: About what?
> Gil: It's about a um…, a man who works in a nostalgia shop.
> Hemingway: What t'hell is a nostalgia shop?
> Gil: Y'know, a place where they sell old things, memorabilia. And, does that sound terrible?
> Hemingway: No subject is terrible if the story is true, if the story is clean and honest, and if it affirms courage and grace under pressure.

For our purposes, the interesting thing about the movie – a movie deeply embedded within a nostalgia not just for the City of Lights but for a far simpler, more authentic, foundational past that's a generation or two removed from us today, what they call "a golden age" – is that the woman in the Paris of the 1920s with whom Gil soon falls in love, Adriana, is herself nostalgic, but for a time that is in *her* immediate past: Paris of the so-called Belle Époque, a period dating from the early 1870s until the start of World War I. And one evening as she strolls with Gil in 1920s Paris, an even earlier horse-drawn carriage (thus not a car this time) pulls up alongside them at midnight, and they magically travel to that past. There they meet famous artists from that earlier era, such as Paul Gaugin and Henri Toulouse-Lautrec, at the once famous bistro, Maxim's.

But it is at this point, the point of dueling golden ages and competing nostalgias (Gil's being the 1920s, Adriana's being a generation before that) that Gil realizes something that he's not previously understood: that nostalgia for a golden age, for a definitive past that anchors the present, a previous moment that then lends meaning to now – in a word, a nostalgia for an origin – is not about the past at all but (as their friend Paul suggested rightly, despite his condescension, at the outset of the film) about the present. As Gil says to Adriana:

> [I]f you stay here, though, and this becomes your present, then pretty soon you'll start imagining another time was really your..., you know, was really the golden time. Yeah, that's what the present is. It's a little unsatisfying because life's a little unsatisfying.

This is the realization that (without spoiling the ending here) leads to Gil returning to the present, rather more content and apparently cured of his golden-age thinking.

The point? The car that picks Gil up isn't vintage until he sees it from his particular vantage point today. Or, to put it another way, it's not about the fossil but, instead, about the frame and the now taken-for-granted (by many but not all) view of geological time that we, in the present, are working with, the narrative that allows us to make sense of time and *see it as* a fossil; so too, it's not about the rock that I passed around class but, instead, about the authority the students lend to me, as their professor, and the discourse on ancient Greece that they walk around with, unknowingly. In much the same way, nostalgia is not about the past, a long-gone time of origins, when our ancestors walked the earth ("Back in the good old days" we sometimes say), but in fact it is all about the present, a present judged dissatisfying only by reference to its inhabitant's ideas of what the past might have been like – a past that, like the standards against which a life is judged, lives nowhere but in our imaginations, here and now, a product of our criteria for what counts as worth living and worth remembering and what's worth forgetting about. These criteria change, of course, which in turn changes judgments and history and alters the origins that we once thought were somewhere out there, far removed from us, the so-called golden age that constitutes the standard against which we are judged. For we now – like Gil – through our discourse on that gray rock, or that "fossil," start to see the significance we attribute to things as being just that, *our* contestable attributions (after all, others, who come with different interests, are doing this too), attributions that tell us far more about ourselves and our situations than about some seemingly tangible, distant past.

It's not an easy shift to make – to see history and origins tales as being all about the tale-teller's present situation, like when an elder at some family get-together says, "Well, when I was a kid..." or when someone accounts for a current practice by saying, "Well, originally, that was used to...." The following twenty chapters, arranged in pairs (the second of each set being a commissioned commentary on, an elaboration of, the first), press this shift but in a variety of different settings (from stories about the good old days to book reviews on amazon.com), modeling how we might complicate the way we so routinely talk about the authoritative past, the time of origins, and how we so often think of the needs of the present as if they had always existed, as if they had been handed, like a relay race's baton, from the past to us today. I think it fair to say that each chapter invites readers to listen carefully to the voice of the one telling the tale of origins, and not to succumb to the romance of their story, forgetting that it is told by someone, at a specific time, in a particular situation, for some effect. For, as Tara Baldrick-Morrone reminds us in her chapter, we must always keep in mind Bruce Lincoln's advice to ask: "Who speaks here?" regardless of how compelling the tale might be. For, as in the case of that little gray rock, we can't forget that no one cared all that much about it until a professor attached a story to it.

Russell T. McCutcheon is Professor and Chair of the Department of Religious Studies at the University of Alabama. His research is about the social and political implications of competing classification systems.

1. Buying Origins

Our Sofas, Ourselves

Leslie Dorrough Smith

I was browsing the internet recently for a new sofa. During my online window-shopping, I came across a stunning magenta number (called the "Swan Sofa") at a popular modern furnishings store, Design Within Reach. The sofa "stuns" not only because of its color, but also because it looks quite different than most run-of-the mill couches: all of its lines are curved and undulating, with no right angles anywhere to be seen, except on its brilliant chrome legs. Here's how the sofa is described online:

> Before the Swan Sofa (1958), Arne Jacobsen's architecture and designs were shaped by an assumption of materials' natural ways of resisting. In other words, he could make them go only so far in becoming the structures he desired. With new technologies, however, the old rules no longer applied, and he was able to shape fluid curves and single-piece molded shells. The Swan Sofa is now made from polyurethane foam, but at the time, Jacobsen used Styropore® to create its continuous shape. Designed for the SAS Royal Hotel in Copenhagen, for which Jacobsen was the architect. A single upholsterer hand-sews the fabric onto the frame of the Swan. Original design and licensed manufacture by Republic of Fritz Hansen. Made in Poland.

Of the myriad ways in which identities are constructed, telling the origins of something often acts as a natural authorizing statement. While many folk might interpret this sofa as nothing more than an object to sit upon, the description above implies that it's part technological wonder, part artistic expression. Rather than any old mass-produced piece of furniture, this is the product of "a single upholsterer['s]" craftsmanship. In short, knowing the origins of this couch – its designer, his background, its first intended function, etc. – validates not only the aesthetic appeal of a magenta sofa (when, to many, something a bit more neutral might seem a better investment), but more than that, it serves as an endorsement of its price (which, in the magenta fabric, is US$7,248.00).

For those of us with smaller pocketbooks, consider how Target's Elliot Sofa Bed is described. Like the previous sofa, it too is brightly rendered (in a crayon orange fabric), with tufting and sleek lines to boot. Unlike the Swan, though, this one is quite angular, in part because it's also a futon and is thus meant to recline completely flat. Also in contrast to the Swan, it retails for US$199.00. Here's its online description:

> Give a bold and interesting look to your living space with the Elliot sofa bed in orange. Perfect for small spaces like studios, lofts and dorm rooms, this innovative futon sofa bed is convertible into 5 different positions for sitting, lounging and sleeping. The citrus hue surprises and delights and will set off virtually anything you pair it with, from soft blue throw pillows to bamboo accent pieces. Made from durable wood and wood composites, the frame features a rich espresso finish to complement the fabric color. Soft microfiber and cotton blend for a durable cover that can be wiped down with a damp cloth for easy cleaning. This convertible sofa bed comes with a 6″ firm mattress with foam filling. The sleeper sofa bed also has comfy cushions that are filled with foam and polyester to give you maximum support and shape.

Notice anything here? While the lengths of the descriptions of the sofas are certainly similar, the Target sofa lacks an origins narrative. There is no presumed insight into the designer's mind, no romanticized story of a café where the sofa's design first entered his/her consciousness and was hastily scribbled onto a crumb-ridden napkin. There are no tales of individual upholsterers and their careful hand-stitching, for we all know that no such person was likely involved in the crafting of this piece. In short, the Target sofa's description is one that lacks a history. Absent the past, it is transformed (comparatively) into a mere commodity, the central selling points of which are "easy cleaning" and "comfy cushions," if what the description indicates is true.

Perhaps it goes without saying that one could partly attribute the price difference between these two products to variances in the quality of the raw materials they use, the precision of the labor involved to create them, etc.; we are not, in fairness, necessarily comparing apples with apples. But unless the frame of the magenta sofa is made of gold, we would be naïve if we did not recognize that we are buying a very expensive story in addition to a piece of furniture. After all, both sofas were made to serve similar practical functions. But because one has had a mythical "life" that the other has not, this claim to an origin of some symbolic value actually ends up providing another sort of value measurable in dollars and cents.

A similar experience often goes on in mid- to higher-end brick and mortar furniture stores as well, where one is not encouraged simply to purchase the sofa off the showroom floor – rather, one may enter a "design center," the name for the portion of the store where the consumer may customize many, if not most, of that sofa's features ("We have over 10,000 fabrics to choose from!"). While on the surface it may seem that this exercise is nothing other than allowing consumers to voice their preferences (patterns or solids?), when viewed more panoramically, these selection processes themselves are narrative-building moments wherein consumers transform the sofa into an extension of themselves. Whether I like nailhead trim or beige over greige may appear to be a mere aesthetic choice; the point, however, is that I am often willing to pay more for the experience of making a sofa precisely what I want it to be. I have paid not just for a particular look, but more generally, for owning something that I can claim is special, unique, or individualized.

Couture and customized sofas aside, the phenomenon at play here is nothing other than the rather ordinary human act of creating a history intended to manufacture distinction, and from that, status. Consider how we daily engage in origin-telling as we trace ourselves back to royalty, tell how we've triumphed over childhood traumas, or even describe what fraction of Native American blood may course through our veins. These are not the only things to tell about ourselves, of course; most of us conveniently omit certain aspects – for instance we don't usually share stories of our persistent skin rashes or alcoholism so willingly. Rather, how we tell stories about ourselves, our religions, our nations, and our families is a process of customization very much like selecting a bold striped fabric or name-dropping the designer of that fabulous chaise lounge. Certain things are forefronted even as others remain in the wings; in this sense, we are searching for selling points in marketing identity. If cultures' origins stories are almost always intended to impart a degree of uniqueness, strength, and authenticity that others simply can't match, then these are never innocent facts, but directly frame how one is to be historicized, contextualized, and from this, valued.

Leslie Dorrough Smith is Assistant Professor of Religious Studies and Chair of the Women's and Gender Studies program at Avila University, Kansas City. Her current research examines the interplay between gender, sex, reproduction, and the politics of American evangelical groups.

Our Stuff, Our Stories

Kat Daley-Bailey

Woody: You gave him my pink shirt? You gave a complete stranger my pink shirt? That pink shirt was a Christmas present from you. I treasured that shirt. I loved that shirt. My collar size has grown a full size from weight lifting. And you saw my arms had grown, you saw my neck had grown. And you bought me that shirt for my new body. I loved that shirt. The first shirt for my new body. And you gave that away. I can't believe it. I hate it here. I hate this house. I hate you. (Guare 1994: 74)

In this episode from the play, *Six Degrees of Separation* by John Guare, a spoiled college-age son of wealthy art dealers explodes in anger and resentment toward his parents because they gave away his pink shirt. This is an example – a rather hyperbolic example – of the type of meaning (via narratives) we instill in inanimate objects. The argument is not really about the pink shirt…but their thoughtless relinquishment of his pink shirt stands as a sign for the son of his parents' disregard for him. Despite the hostility of his words, this encounter represents a moment of levity in the play, a rabid critique of privilege and a challenge to a cultural status quo regarding the value or worth of something or someone. We might respond that "it is just a shirt," an inanimate object, and yet we too often react in similar ways when it comes to the objects with which we surround ourselves. Woody has imbued his pink shirt with significance and value far beyond its economic value. He is not upset at his parents primarily because the shirt was expensive but rather *that it held a special value for him*. So whether the object in question is a shirt or a sofa, we can be sure that both individually and socially we construct stories about ourselves and our society by tethering various meanings and values to the objects we may possess.

A sofa has many practical functions; it is a place to sit, to entertain guests, a spot to stretch out on, or to lie down and sleep or think, to watch TV, play video games, etc. Sitting furniture comes in multiple forms which speak to a wide range of functionality, physically and socially (the love seat, the Ottoman, the Lazy-Boy, etc.). Take, for example, the rich velvet "fainting couches" of the Victorian era: their odd shape (that of a long couch with a raised back on only one side) demonstrates they were designed for a single person to recline upon. Owning a fainting couch today might suggest an affinity with certain social classes of a particular historical period (i.e., the nineteenth century) in which tightly corseted upper-class women required specific sitting structures, couches that undoubtedly many modern middle-class Americans today would deem impractical, uncomfortable, and superfluous. To such consumers, a fainting couch may be, at best, a relic of times past, an item for collecting but certainly not a piece of practical furniture. But the fainting couch in its day did function, socially, in a very particular and meaningful way. It provided a marker of class status in a time when class was not dictated purely by net worth but hinged a great deal on bloodlines, cultural heritage, as well as a type of competency in social minutia. Owning such an expensive piece of furniture that didn't actually perform a vital physical function was an individual's way of tapping into a narrative of social exclusivity.

One might compare ownership of a fainting couch today to owning the first sofa presented in Smith's chapter, the Swan Sofa. Part of its allure is that it is not practical; but then again, the social function of the Swan Sofa is to set the owner apart from the masses, to suggest the owner's good taste and cultural pedigree. The origins story of the first sofa presents it as a work of art, something hand-crafted and rare. If the sofa's value lies not in its ability to function as a comfortable seat, what is its function? What justifies a 7,248-dollar price tag?

Its social function is to engage the viewer in a system of signs, to provide the owner with a script to share with visitors, a script that recounts the object's miraculous creation (the elaborate origins narrative cited in Smith's piece). Via the incantation of this particular origins narrative the Swan Sofa magically becomes the incarnation of a famous architect's genius, an embodiment of a royal hotel's aesthetic, and a material rendering of mankind's innate desire to mimic the gods' primordial acts of creation. Without this orienting narrative wildly gesturing toward the transcendent ideals that, it suggests, are inherent in this sofa, the Swan Sofa merely provides a place to sit. But this story isn't really about the sofa, is it? Just as Woody's meltdown is not really about the pink shirt itself but rather what the pink shirt symbolizes to him, the Swan Sofa's advertisement suggests *that it represents much more.* According to this accounting of social signs via the advertisement's narrative, the owner's worth is clearly demon-strated in this piece of fluidly shaped, and extremely expensive, foam.

While some sofa buyers might suggest that comfort, affordability, and sustainability are the most desired properties buyers seek in furniture, one is quickly disabused of this notion in this particular case. Recognition of the innate value of such a piece of art acts as a type of litmus test or secret handshake among the social elite. The narrative allows both the owner and the visitor to be participants in the arbitration of the sofa's, and owner's, value and worth.

Now, before we dismiss the first sofa's description as merely superficial and pandering to elite tastes, we should delve into the narrative presented in the second sofa's description. Both sofas have stories. Both narratives are meant to project a particular viewing of the object to the consumer. Both narratives are suggesting that there is something beyond the material, in this case beyond the two sofas displayed before us. The second sofa's narrative does appear to engage the buyer at a functional level but it lacks an origins story, a birth narrative about how exactly the sofa came into being. Amassing the various descriptors in the narrative allows readers to systematically uncover the previously obfuscated elements of the narrative. The cushions are "comfy" but also provide support. This sofa is "bold" and "interesting." Its orange color, that some would find jarring, is described as a "citrus hue" which "surprises and delights." It is made of "durable" wood. That wood is not described as merely brown but as a "rich espresso." It sounds inviting and aromatic, doesn't it? What is being sold in this narrative is not just bits of wood, foam and polyester but, rather, the ideal of convenience, comfort, and an anticipatory future of impromptu sleepovers, with "surprised and delighted" guests lounging in one's studio, loft, or dorm room, drinking delicious "rich espresso" and having "bold" and "interesting" conversations, all the while nestled among the "comfy" cushions of your new Elliot Sofa Bed.

So while the first sofa's narrative sells an origins narrative suggestive of worth and artistic good taste, the second sofa's narrative is an anticipatory one which implies that this piece of furniture assists you in creating a world – your world. Decorating is the new mode of self-expression for the first world masses. As its narrative suggests, the Elliot Sofa Bed offers consumers multiple possibilities but it is you, the consumer, whose individual choices (whether you live in a studio, loft, or dorm room, no matter which of the five different positions you utilize, or what you pair the sofa with, be it "soft blue accent pillows" or "bamboo accent pieces") create your world. You are master of your own decorative destiny. This narrative champions a type of consumer agency in which individuals are free – free to consume. Also, as the Target narrative steers buyers toward an allusive type of consumer agency, it obfuscates the actual processes by which such goods are produced, hence no origins narrative.

Perhaps Target does not wish to advertise the origins narrative of its products. Perhaps its origins narrative might lead us to facts that consumers would find unsavory and would rather remain ignorant of (think factories in third world countries, undesirable working conditions, etc.). Many retailers have plugged into the fair-trade movement and, therefore, place their origins narratives front and center in their advertisement campaigns (assuaging first world guilt while encouraging moral smugness among their customers) or have adopted a made-in-America branding system, thereby tapping into American nationalist rhetoric to encourage buyers. Others, like the sellers of the Swan Sofa, Design Within Reach, invest in narratives of exclusivity and artistic mysticism to market their products. Target's Elliot Sofa Bed was not created ex nihilo, out of nothing. Perhaps buyers should therefore be just as wary of the absence of an origins narrative as of one's inclusion.

Kat Daley-Bailey received a Master's degree in the study of religion from the University of Georgia in 2004, and taught courses for ten years at Georgia State University, Georgia Perimeter College, and the University of Georgia. Since Summer 2014, she has taken a full-time position as academic advisor at the University of Georgia.

2. Techniques of Then and Now

When the Stakes are High

Vaia Touna

In her chapter, "Our Sofas, Ourselves," on how we all resort to telling origins stories, Leslie Dorrough Smith notes that it's a common rhetorical technique used when selling products and when talking about ourselves, either as individuals or as group members of nations, religions, etc. No doubt we do tell origins stories and create myths to prove our worth: "I was here first!" says the little kid when competing for the swing.

But what Smith's chapter made me think of is why and when we give way to this technique. For it seems to me that individuals and groups succumb to this rhetorical technique to secure a certain position – whether that is to gain a status of worthiness in relation to a friend, among family members, or as groups in relation to other groups – when the maintenance of the status is either fragile or, as with kids at the swing, threatened by another challenger (real or imagined). We therefore, I think, use this technique when the stakes are high, and this is something to which I would like to give a little more attention.

To return to Smith's example of the way we use narratives to sell sofas, the stakes are apparently different between the Design Within Reach and Target stores, not only in terms of the group they're each aiming at (their potential customers), but also in relation to the different spaces in competing markets that each store tries to occupy. In the case of Design Within Reach the status it holds is likely more fragile and competitive and therefore there is a stronger need to not just sell a "good" product but also to dress it with a story that sounds worth telling (and therefore worth selling/buying). An origins discourse thus regulates competitive economies of identity and status.

To take the above syllogism a bit further, I would say that origins tales and mythic narratives of glorious pasts (not to forget, of course, discourses on tradition as well), are in fact used more often by members of nations that are under crisis (whether political, economic, etc.). That is, when the stakes are high and the need to maintain or gain a certain social status (and the benefits that follow) is of immense importance. Borders of nations are thus maintained, identities are therefore united and distinguished; claims of origins, lineage, and traditions serve, after all, as the common denominator.

To return yet again to Smith's example, companies such as Design Within Reach therefore try to sell not just a product but a lifestyle as well, that will unite their customers not only in terms of owning a (no doubt) very expensive product but also as members now of an imagined community with a certain social/economic status. The resort to this technique thus seems simultaneously to reinforce the membership's coherence on the one hand, while on the other ensuring this group has a more beneficial status vis-à-vis other groups.

But surely this is not a simple process and a great many apparatuses are turning their wheels to make these stories successful (i.e., effective). Think about the considerable amount of money that Design Within Reach no doubt invests on board meetings and discussions, assigning the advertising experts to come up with a variety of stories from which the board will choose the one that will eventually make their product (and the lifestyle and identity that apparently come with it) a commodity worth valuing and buying. Of course, the investment doesn't stop here; for an origins story to be successful there needs to be constant tweaking, changing it according to consumer tastes, interests, and needs – which are themselves always changing. Therefore, the stakes are always high.

Vaia Touna is an Assistant Professor in the Department of Religious Studies at the University of Alabama. Her research focuses on the sociology of identity formation with examples drawn from ancient to modern Greece.

High Stakes on the High Court

Michael Graziano

In the past few years, the United States Supreme Court has taken on a number of high-profile cases. Whether the issue is guns (*District of Columbia v. Heller* [2008]), healthcare (*NFIB v. Sebelius* [2012]), or same-sex marriage (*United States v. Windsor* [2013]), the justices have embraced cases that have high-stake implications for American law. Though dealing with different issues, each case relied upon appeals to the historical origins of the Constitution – in theory, the supreme law of the land in the US – in order to determine what rulings should be made in the present.

Supreme Court justices are in many ways rigorously self-reflexive about their role in the legal process. They are less self-reflexive, however, when it comes to history. For when it comes to history, many on the Court are frequent fliers to what Russell McCutcheon, in the introduction to this volume, terms "this foreign land called 'the past' where origins are thought to reside." Of interest to a study of origins is how the Court *produces the very evidence which it seeks to analyze*. Since the Court's job is to determine what is lawful according the Constitution, the history of the Court's decisions makes its own case, so to speak, about what the Constitution *really* is and what it means.

In the Supreme Court, American history is singular; the United States has one origin – the Constitution. This is why fights over the *right* history are so important: the One True Origin is a trump card in legal debates in the Court.

Justice Antonin Scalia has been the staunchest defender of this approach. Scalia calls himself an "originalist," by which he means that the job of the Court is to apply *the* original understanding of the Constitution, that is, what the text was thought to mean at the time it was written. As Scalia said at an appearance in 2005, "I have my rules that confine me. I'm looking for the original meaning and when I find it I am handcuffed," before adding, tongue-in-cheek, "I cannot do all the mean conservative things I would love to do to this society" (Talbot 2005). The image of Scalia as handcuffed to the "past" is a seductive one for those who agree with his originalist position, and a troubling vision for those who view him as a subversive on the highest court in the land. Judging from media accounts, depending on which side of the aisle one calls home (after all, there are supposedly only two), history is either defended or eviscerated in the hands of Justice Scalia. You could be forgiven for mistaking Scalia for a spirit medium, channeling the past at a whim. For Scalia, what the Court is deciding in recent cases is not whether it should be legal to, say, own a handgun in the District of Columbia or legally bind oneself in marriage to someone with similar genitalia, but whether the Constitution – *as originally written* – was ever meant to do such a thing in the first place. Scalia claims that it is not his own interests which guide his decisions, but rather what the Constitution *originally meant*. The justice explains that he sometimes has to vote against his own personal opinion, since that's what the Constitution demands. An interviewer's dream, he has a knack for explaining himself in such a way as to give his liberal counterparts aneurysms: "A lot of stuff that's stupid is not unconstitutional. I gave a talk once where I said they ought to pass out to all federal judges a stamp, and the stamp says – Whack! [Pounds his fist.] – STUPID BUT CONSTITUTIONAL. Whack!" (Senior 2013).

Stupid but, since history has spoken, constitutional. This is because, as Scalia explains, the Constitution is a series of words. "Words have meaning. And their meaning doesn't change," Scalia explains – using a contraction ("doesn't") that did not exist before 1739 (according to Merriam-Webster, the first known usage of "doesn't" occurred in this year). Of course, there are exceptions. Americans acknowledge that the framers of the Constitution owned and bred human beings as slaves, yet contemporary justices tend not to see that as relevant when deciding cases today. It is understood that *that* narrative of the past is no longer important for adjudicating laws. Some differences make a difference. Of course, the story of slavery – or the lack of it in some origins stories about the Constitution – is itself a particular kind of origins narrative. The trick is in the telling: apparently, one needs to know when all men are created equal, and when all men are not.

In other words, context matters. What one chooses to leave out of one particular origins story – the role of human slavery in shaping a particular document – and what one chooses to put in another particular origins story – say, the manufacturing history of a couch – is but one strategy to shape a particular origin for a particular need. Originalism is the strategy of telling stories to determine winners and losers, and this strategy is certainly not confined to the bench. Historians and others who critique "law office history" seem to suggest that what is aggrieved in these situations is *history*, since it is history that is being made to enable (erroneously, unjustly) particular actions in the present.

Yet Vaia Touna's approach provides us with a way to reframe both the critics and their critiques. For it would seem that these self-appointed defenders of the past are engaged in much the same process as the justices of whose history they seem to think so little. Both the justices and the historians who critique them presume the past has within it the blueprint for the future. Touna pokes and prods at the soft underbelly of such a critique. The critics, Touna might suggest, seem to lose sight of the fact that originalism is a strategy directed toward a particular end, and that end is not historical truth – whatever *that* is. Rather than seeing the debate between Scalia and his critics as one over whose past is wrong, we should instead envision this as a dispute very much anchored in the present – say, a dispute over the distribution of cultural, political, and economic power by a state apparatus with the power to enforce its decrees. When Scalia is knocked for being incoherent, then, the critique seems to amount to little more than the acknowledgment that he values different things differently in different contexts. To put it another way: specific origins serve specific needs.

So origins stories are about state power, yes, but they are also about a great deal else – such as selling couches. It may seem a bit melodramatic, after talking about handguns and healthcare, to think of origins stories in terms of selling furniture, but that is *precisely* where Touna's approach becomes most useful since it serves as a reminder that we tell origins stories in *any* situation when the stakes are perceived as high. One does not have to serve on the US Supreme Court to be an originalist. Touna suggests that origins stories are a signal of everyday tension, of the status quo in distress. Appealing to origins can operate as a rhetorical WD-40, a handy lubricant to loosen those parts of the past that we need most and make sure they don't squeak too loudly when put to work in the present. It is the difference between being handcuffed *to* the past and shackled *in* the past.

Michael Graziano is a PhD candidate in the Religion Department at Florida State University. His dissertation explores the relationship between American intelligence agencies and religious institutions during the Cold War.

3. Pick a Past, Any Past

The Politics of Choice

Craig Martin

George Washington's Sacred Fire (2006) – in which Peter A. Lilback argues that "founding father" George Washington was a Christian and not a deist – garnered a great deal of media attention when first published. On amazon.com the book currently enjoys 165 user reviews, from readers asserting that the book is "awesome" and "indispencible" [sic] to readers asserting that the book is "illegitimate," "junk," and "propaganda." Why does it matter if George Washington was a deist or a Christian? What's at stake in the application of one of these two labels onto a figure long dead?

From the book's description and the positive reviews it enjoys, the answer is readily apparent: for some readers, a Christian George Washington should serve as an ongoing "inspirational" model for United States' leaders and for a "Christian nation" as a whole. Consider the following reviewer's claims (spelling and punctuation all original):

> George Washington was a man of honor and this book brings that out. We need another President like him.

> All these haters because it has conservative points of view? Guess what, our founding fathers were more conservative than all but a handfull of republicans. We're becoming a "sissy version" of what we once were.

> [Washington's] devout belief in Divine Providence as it relates to the founding of this nation was unshakable. An inspiration to anyone who has even just one patriotic bone in their body.

> Makes you want to be involved in taking America back from the lying looting thugs!!

> Our contempary congress should take a clue from him.

Good for the kids to read inorder for them to know why America was founded and why we need GOD back in our country.

George Washington, the father of our nation must be in turmoil over what we have done to our nation. His moral character, and dependence on our holy father, Jesus, made him the man he was. We have much to learn and much to do to come within a mile of this mans integrity.

Clearly, for many readers this book serves as a useful moral guide and a return-to-origins narrative. The US has gotten away from its authentic, Christian origins – modeled by Washington – and we must turn away from our corrupt detours and return to Washington's ideal.

Of course, two (or ten) can play at this game. I often see people who don't identify as Christian post the following quote on Facebook, sometimes with a picture of George Washington above it:

As the Government of the United States of America is not, in any sense, founded on the Christian religion; as it has in itself no character of enmity against the laws, religion, or tranquillity, of Mussulmen; and, as the said States never entered into any war, or act of hostility against any Mahometan nation, it is declared by the parties, that no pretext arising from religious opinions, shall ever produce an interruption of the harmony existing between the two countries.

The quotation is not, however, from Washington; it was written by Joel Barlow, approved by the United States Senate, and signed in 1797 by then-president John Adams. But the quotation seems to serve the same purpose: it proposes an alternative origin to the American nation – this time a non-Christian origin – that presumably is to serve as an ongoing model for American politics or policies.

Interestingly, the question of whether America is Christian and, if so, opposed to Islam, is raised by one of the reviewers of *Sacred Fire* who writes,

We are not and never were a Muslim nation even though Pres. Obama said "if you actually took the number of Muslim Americans, we'd be one of the largest Muslim countries in the world."
False statement!!!!
Obama said in Turkey that Americans "do not consider ourselves a Christian nation."
What is he talking about? The idea that the United States is a "Christian nation," has always been central to American identity. The majority of Americans (73–76%) identify themselves as Christians.

What we have are two competing visions of America, then: one according to which there is nothing Christian about America and, therefore, nothing intrinsically at odds with Islam; another according to which America is intrinsically Christian and, therefore, there might presumably be something wrong with the estimated number of Muslims in America.

Of course, none of this gets to how the readers in question define "Christianity" or "deism" (or "Islam," for that matter). One reader of *Sacred Fire* suggests that, despite Lilback's assumption that "Christian" and "deist" are mutually exclusive, this could be a "false dichotomy" and it's possible that Washington could have used both identifiers simultaneously. Another reviewer suggests that the author of the book deploys an anachronistic portrayal of what counts as "Christian": "The TESTS of being a real Christian are based on their 21st Century Evangelical definitions of a Christian." Not only is the definition of "America" at stake here, but so is the definition of "Christianity." Perhaps Lilback's next book will be on the so-called historical Jesus, in order settle that question for his readers.

Such return to origins games require a process of selection; even if Washington was "Christian" – whatever that means – it's nevertheless clear that not everything associated with Washington will continue to serve as a model for *modern* America. For instance, Washington owned slaves, but I doubt any of the readers who offered five-star reviews of the book would want to resurrect slavery. So which parts of Washington's life – or, rather, what we can project backward in time as his "life" – will be selected as our ongoing model? Of course the answer to this question depends on individual readers' sympathies.

Craig Martin is an Associate Professor of Religious Studies at St Thomas Aquinas College, Sparkill, NY. His research focuses on theory and method in the study of religion.

The Origins Games

Karen deVries

In "The Politics of Choice" Craig Martin enacts a particular approach to the study of religion that may at first seem counter-intuitive. He begins with a story about a contested history: was George Washington a Christian or a deist? This question quickly turns out to be connected to an origins story – whether or not the United States was *originally* founded as a Christian nation. Instead of jumping into the fray and taking sides about which story is more accurate, Martin views them from a different angle and describes them as "origins games" in which all sides use rhetorical tactics and strategies. Like a sportscaster analyzing and reporting the moves of players on a field, he provides details to make the game more vivid before concluding with a few provocative statements. To highlight Martin's methodology, I offer first a retelling of his story about these other stories.

The central game in Martin's story follows two teams who have competing visions of America. Let's call them Team Conservative Christianity and Team Liberal Tolerance. Playing for Team Conservative Christianity, we have a selection of book reviewers on amazon.com who are proud fans of long-ago deceased star player, George Washington. Let's call him GW. The first reviewer thinks GW is the greatest player in the history of players. A second reviewer thinks people who don't like GW are "sissies." A few other reviewers think contemporary players could and should learn a lot from GW because he played the game the way they think it ought to be played. In Martin's story, GW's fans mostly hang out on Amazon.

Over on Facebook, Martin finds a few people who are rooting for Team Liberal Tolerance with a quote attributed to GW stating that the United States is not founded on Christian religion. It turns out, however, that they have made the rather embarrassing error of confusing GW with John Adams. Although Adams also played during GW's golden era, he doesn't have quite as much star power. Returning to Amazon to find additional commentary, Martin references a cadre of folks who have some concerns about whether or not Team Christianity is using the correct definition of "Christian." Mistaken identities and definitional disputes aside, we now have a picture of the two teams and their shared strategy – that is, they both authorize their competing visions for present-day America by appealing to a past authoritative figure.

Having provided highlights from this particular origins game and pointed out the strategy shared by the opposing teams, Martin concludes his essay with a provocative statement about the mechanics of this common tactic. It requires, he tells us, a process of selection in which decisions are made about *how* to tell GW's story so that it appears to be a good model. Less savory details about GW's life, such as his willing participation in and promotion of an economy dependent on legalized ownership of black bodies, have been left out of Team Conservative Christianity's tale. Though Martin does not pursue this path, one might imagine this is the kind of detail that could work as ammunition for Team Tolerance in its efforts to fabricate an alternative origins story and concomitant vision for America.

As the games rage on, Martin's story winds down and might perhaps leave the reader wondering how, or if, he is himself implicated in the tale. What is the role of the scholar confronted with another stirring round of origins games? One might be tempted to sit back, pass the popcorn, and see who throws the next origin story. For those of us wanting more nourishment than popcorn, Martin's concluding sentence points us in a productive direction. When fabricating origins stories, storytellers choose threads of narratives to weave new origins stories that align with what Martin calls "individual readers' sympathies." What does this provocative statement about sympathies mean and where might it lead us?

In his foreword to *Religious Truth: A Volume in the Comparative Religious Ideas Project* (Neville [ed.] 2000), the prominent historian of religion, Jonathan Z. Smith, points out that the English word "truth" is etymologically related to the word "trust" insofar as they both share a root word, a botanical noun denoting "tree" and the qualities of wood such as solidity, durability, steadfastness, and trustworthiness. Although etymology can quickly turn into yet another origins game, it can also be used to imagine creative interpretive possibilities. Following the latter route, I propose that we think of what Martin calls "individual readers' sympathies" as a relationship between the origins story and the reception of that story as authoritative. Readers inclined to be persuaded by a particular version of a story are those who trust that the story (and its fabricator) conveys something they might call "the truth" or statements about the world that they consider reliable. Individuals sympathize with those they trust, and those one trusts are typically those perceived as protecting or advancing one's interests in the game of life.

Now our story has two games: the origins game and the game of life. In this framework, the origins game comes into view as a spectacle. For critical theorists, the spectacle demands analysis. What kind of work does the spectacle do? Who or what does it serve? What fantasies and desires does it tap into? What might it be distracting our attention from? What other kinds of stories might we tell about the spectacle? And what are the politics of choice for those who find themselves caught up in these games? These are just some questions critical scholars of religion might pursue.

In her 2008 science fiction novel, *The Hunger Games*, Suzanne Collins provides an alternative story about a spectacle and the game of life. It takes place in a dystopian future America called Panem where the wealthy metropolis, The Capitol, exercises political control over the country's twelve districts by hosting an annual Hunger Games. Through a lottery, each district "chooses" one boy and one girl to compete as tributes against each other in a televised battle to the death. In the poorer districts, extra food rations may be obtained by adding a child's name to the lottery multiple times. For these folks and their loved ones, the games reinforce their powerlessness against the Capitol's brutal control of resources. The wealthier districts, however, view the games as entertaining sport as they train up their youth for the exciting possibility of being chosen as a tribute.

In Collins' story, the possible options that fans and players might "choose" depend entirely on where they are situated, but these elements do not constitute the primary action of the story. The action instead focuses on the tributes' struggles to survive in a world where they become part of the spectacle that reinforces the status quo even as it distracts attention from the grossly disproportionate distribution of resources that structure the material realities for viewers across Panem. While *The Hunger Games* does not have anything to say about religious identifications, it provides some ideas for scholars thinking about spectacle as a product of power relations.

In the origins games spectacle, fans and players on Team Conservative Christianity and Team Liberal Tolerance spar over whether or not one of America's "Founding Fathers" was a Christian or a deist as they fabricate origins stories authorizing their versions of the status quo. Having identified this key rhetorical strategy, a scholar of religion might then turn her analytic focus toward the conditions that create the spectacle. What kind of norms legitimize those who not only essentialize but also denigrate femaleness so that a term like "sissy" automatically registers as an insult? What structures of power view non-white bodies as resources to be managed and exploited for labor? Given the racial configuration of mass incarceration today, this question is as relevant to ask of contemporary politicians as it is to understanding George Washington's context. For those of us witnesses of and participants in spectacles of suffering, pursuing such questions might help us find our way out of the origins games into fresher air where action in the game of life is not a fantasy of the past but a reality happening right here and now.

Karen deVries received her PhD from the History of Consciousness Department at the University of California, Santa Cruz, and she is a lecturer in the Political Science Department of Montana State University. Her research combines religion studies, science and technology studies, feminist theory, critical race studies, and queer theory to analyze contemporary religious/secular binaries.

4. Selling Identities

One Coffee Bean at a Time

Monica R. Miller

During a recent coffee run at Starbucks, an advertisement caught my eye. Written on a matte black background, in a font graphically validating any hipster toting around a typewriter, it read:

> Ethiopia Single-Origin: Velvety-soft with peppery spice and sweet citrus notes.

Many things about this ad struck me as curious, not to mention that I was a bit put off by the assumption that my academic palate could ascertain or care to find the "citrus notes" of a coffee bean. But I began to *imagine* that there was more being sold here than just coffee. So I began to question. Does "origin" have reference to the coffee bean, or to the drinker? Does "single" indicate that the coffee beans all hail from individual, specific locales? Do coffee beans have a sense of geography and transnational borders? Is the nod to "Ethiopia" about the bean or an arrow pointing in the direction of a suggested consumer? Would someone from Ethiopia walk into this café and immediately feel at home-away-from-home? Most curious to me were the ways in which "origin" as a single and monolithic thing was juxtaposed over and against the country Ethiopia which is, like all nations, as heterogeneous inside its borders as it is arbitrary in terms of those borders. Waiting on my café Americano – I wasn't sold by the ad – I began to think that "Ethiopia" and "Single-Origin" coupled to create a homogenizing effect through mythological constructions of singularity and originality.

They were selling me an identity.

Sitting in the coffee shop, I couldn't help but imagine global cultural flows transmuting into a brackish water of coffee and identity. I was spurred on by the global commodity that I was enjoying, as much as by the way an "act of identification" was being marketed through a mash-up of sameness and difference on a sign, a sign about coffee. What could possibly be singular about the country Ethiopia and the coffee beans produced there? Consider, for example, that in Ethiopia there are over ninety individual languages/communication systems operative. Just a brief consideration of the (cross-cultural and geographical) travel involved in the producing, manufacturing, and selling of commodities like coffee beans from *this* place and *that* ought to shift such discourse on the perceived distinctiveness of such claims. But the effect seems to be produced as much through a simple concession to the origins of Ethiopian coffee beans, as from the disjuncture between this country and my location in the coffee shop, and the impossibility of ever finding an origin, either here or in Ethiopia. That's why origins are fabricated, after all. Surely, a coffee shop constitutes a site of cultural expression and affinity, and those expressions and "acts of identification" structuring and structured by them are very fluid, porous, and contestable. But in their contestability – and here's where caffeinated brackish water rises – the mythological constructions of singularity and originality are no less singular or originary.

But who could I tell that the coffee shop had it all wrong? Could I turn to the next in line and warn them that they'd be buying into a fabrication? Or are imagined identities able to be told of their own origins? In a well-known passage, Arjun Appadurai notes that

> the imagination has become an organized field of social practices, a form of work (in the sense of both labor and culturally organized practice), and a form of negotiation between sites of agency (individuals) and globally defined fields of possibility. This unleashing of the imagination links the play of pastiche (in some settings) to the terror and coercion of states and their competitors. (Appadurai 2006: 587)

This manufactured (and marketed) sleight of hand helps to produce a compelling illusion of cultural authenticity based in and on a fabrication of a certain sort of mythological past that can be consumed in the present without accounting for (a wide variety of) change over time and space. Registering the processes of such acts of identification as *acts* – and our claims to origins as imaginary – may be of limited return in a market-driven climate where marketers have stopped selling commodities, or even "cohesive" cultures, but sell identities themselves, a hodge-podge of global cultural flows that are as imaginary as the social imaginary such identities help to constitute. What wakes us up in the morning – caffeine, or the sense of origin, place, space, and identity enacted by the purchase and sipping of an Ethiopian Single-Origin, or in my case, a Café Americano?

So, come sample coffee ground and brewed *here*, made from coffee beans of *that* place over *there*, but purchased right *here* with the swipe of a card. Again, the brackish water.

It seems to me that claims of origins always provide the starting point for *a new discourse of origins* based on prior claims of origination, such that origins tales about the past are used and re-used in the always changing present to create *new claims of beginnings* which in the future will be posited as "The" originary point for yet another new discourse on authenticity. And so on…as each time a new (origins) narrative takes its place, where there were once others, and the cycle begins again.

How do *you* study origins narratives? Asked differently, where and when are your coffee beans grown?

Monica R. Miller is Assistant Professor of Religion and Africana Studies at Lehigh University in Bethlehem, Pennsylvania. Her research considers the intersections of religion in youth culture, popular culture, identity and difference, and theory and method in the study of black religions.

Marketing Christian Roots

Steffen Führding

In January 2007, I was sitting, not at a Starbucks, but with a cup of tea at my IKEA kitchen table, when the headline of a newspaper article drew my attention. In bold black letters I read that Angela Merkel, German chancellor then and now, was looking for Christian references in the constitutional treaty of the European Union that was being discussed at that time. As I learned right at the beginning of the article, the German chancellor had made the following observation:

> I would have wished for a clearer acknowledgment of the *Christian roots*....

I did not continue reading much further, as a whole series of questions, shooting through my head, occupied my attention while reading this statement. Why did Merkel express this wish? Should Europe, or rather the European Union (which ultimately was at the core of the debate), have Christian roots? And what about the still widespread theory of (western) Europe as the last bastion of secularization? How did this idea – advocated not only by scholars but by a majority of citizens, shaping their self-perception of being "the" Europeans – correlate with Merkel's wish?

Naturally, this was not an impromptu statement by Chancellor Merkel; rather, it was part of a much larger debate, which had been ongoing for several years already at that point. Sipping my cup of tea, I thought about this statement, trying to frame it in a larger context and to answer several of my own questions.

The last question – what Europe actually is – or, in fact, the reflections that have been recorded to answer this question, already fill rows and rows of library shelves. What looks so simple on a world map does not appear so clear on closer inspection. Looking at the history of the term "Europe," one is directed to the mythical female figure Europa. Said to be the daughter of a Phoenician king, she was abducted by the father of gods, Zeus, and taken to the isle we call Crete nowadays. Her name was originally used for the region of the Peloponnesian peninsula and was later applied to the entire region north of the Mediterranean. Thus the name of a mythical figure was transferred to a geographical space. However, even today there is no consensus on where the actual geographical borders are situated.

Other attempts at designation refer to a common history or culture, but that does not simplify the situation. It has to be noted that the northern part of the region that we call Europe today was not in contact with "the" ancient Greek and Roman cultures – those cultures designated as representing the origins of Europe – until the nineteenth century. Similarly, this is applicable for the Christianization of Europe, which was very different in the east than in the west. For this Christianization did not happen contemporaneously; it took more than a thousand years until the entirety of what we today know as Europe was, more or less, Christian – whatever this means. And yet Merkel chose to speak of the Christian roots of Europe!

Even though the term "Europe" was known, it was not established or accepted within intellectual circles until the fifteenth century – at a time when the "Turkish threat" dominated the discourse and the Americas were "discovered." (I will refer back to the so-called Turkish threat later.) In fact, it took about 300 years until the term came into common use. Today, it is synonymous with the European Union, which is seen as representative of a unified Europe.

The terms and the ideas of both the Union and Europe alike were never undisputed; designation and definition attempts were manifold and not always uncontroversial. But this is exciting from my point of view. If one does not take part in the attempts at defining and seeing Europe as a coherent, unified entity, but rather focuses on this discourse itself, the category "Europe" can be taken into account as a social and cognitive tool. A tool which can be used to classify the world surrounding us and thus make it interpretable and controllable.

When the Ottomans began threatening the Byzantine Empire at the beginning of the fifteenth century, an attempt was made to create a common "us" by using the category "Europe" in order to separate from, and ward off, that "Turkish threat" (i.e., the "others"). At this point the European discourses and the discourses on the *Christian occident* mingle. Angela Merkel and like-minded people today join in this discourse when they call for an acknowledgment of "Christian roots in Europe" (even though they would never admit it). But why is the chancellor doing this 500 years after the fall of Constantinople? Perhaps because Europe – or, to be more precise, the European Union – is under threat again. For it is in the midst of a profound transformation process, its approval is waning, and its discursive legitimization is brittle.

Since 1989 the question concerning what Europe (here, again, to be understood as the European Union) is supposed to be has been raised more frequently. Two aspects appear to be central to it:

1. With the collapse of the Soviet Union and the end of the east-west conflict, a constitutive element of the self-definition of the European community as distinct from the adversary system in the east disappeared virtually overnight. The idea of the democratic system and the hope for peace and prosperity in a unified Europe, which was so attractive for many central and eastern European nations after the collapse of the Soviet Union, was, for the majority of the western European nations already – at least more or less – a reality and had therefore lost its attraction. These ideas no longer sufficed as the sole core around which to organize an idea of a unified society.

2. Alongside the contemporary historical turn, the economic integration of the European Union had reached its end in the late 1980s. The economic project was concluded; meanwhile, however, the political integration had not kept up step-by-step. Therefore, the wish to make the Union not only a legal-economic space but also a political union started a process of profound transformation.

This is, at least, a widespread interpretation, which I think is not completely wrong. If one applies the theory of social formation to the European Union, one can say that the Union has long been (and still is) on its way into a residual phase. This means that, in its present situation, the Union is no longer capable of reproducing its authority and legitimacy, and the former rhetorical tools (e.g., union of peace and prosperity for all) are now stretched beyond their limits. Thus new (and, in this case, old) tools have to be applied. The discourse of the "Christian occident" is therefore a discursive strategy used in the attempt to streamline and hold together this spacious and heterogeneous form of society.

But isn't there more at play? Is it pure coincidence that this discourse appears to gain momentum at the exact moment of the EU opening negotiations with the Turkey as a possible member state – a country which is often portrayed as "a Muslim nation," at least from the so-called "European point-of-view"? Thus, another discursive strategy comes into the conversation: the discourse of a "secular Europe." This strategy can then be used against modern Turkey, for a religiously classified nation does not fit with the secular west. But even the idea of a secular Europe is not a neutral description, though many Europeans – whatever they may be – understand themselves or the EU as secular. Rather, the discourse on secular Europe is another strategy to uphold and legitimize this supposedly unified form of society.

Ultimately, both narratives – though they seem contradictory, with one being about religion and the other about its absence – are actually two sides of the same discourse. For this is not a matter of the Christian origins of Europe, nor is it about the secular character of the Union. The matter at hand is, instead, about nation-building. On the one hand, there is the creation of a common "us" in distinction to a "them," while on the other hand there is an attempt to give Europe a warm and moralistic appearance in reference to some transcendent all-inclusive values and roots. What is disguised (or is attempted to be disguised – because the attempt to craft a constitution for Europe has failed by now, making it all rather evident) is the disagreement and friction. While the public discusses non-material values, a neo-liberal and capitalist Europe, which is mostly concerned with free markets, is continuously developing. At least since the financial crisis of 2008, the population of southern and southeastern European nations can tell you a thing or two about that.

Thus, for the last time: what is it about when Angela Merkel calls for an acknowledgment of Christian roots in Europe? Like Monica Miller writes above, it is about selling identity. It is meant to transcend material differences and to build up a specific form of society by recovering apparently shared origins.

Steffen Führding works as a Research Assistant and Instructor at the Department for the Study of Religions, Leibniz University, Hannover (Germany) and recently completed his doctoral dissertation. His areas of interest include the history of *Religionswissenschaft* (religious studies) and the role of "religious" rhetoric in identity construction.

5. We Are What We Choose to Recall

Remember the Ala-what-now?

K. Merinda Simmons

Anniversaries are weird. If you don't find yourself wearing an awkward party hat and singing, you're sitting at some ceremony where some officiate or other is telling you that the only way to understand the present is to appreciate the past, or some such cliché. When people talk about a particular day being important because of what happened on that same calendar date however many years ago, I get a little stumped. I can't figure out why the calendar rollover is what brings something or someone to mind. Seems kind of arbitrary. Or, let me put it this way: what and how people remember appear to say way more about the person or people remembering than they do about the "thing itself" that is being remembered.

I'll use a recent event at my home institution as an example. Depending on your interests and/or taste for trivia, June 11 might stand out because it marks Ben Franklin's invention of his Franklin stove in 1742, the patent of a gas-driven automobile in 1895, the adoption of the Puerto Rican flag in 1891, or the release of Hitchcock's first film in 1928 (thanks, internet). The University of Alabama held its own commemorative event, marking the fiftieth anniversary of the school's 1963 desegregation with the enrollment of Vivian Malone and James Hood, as well as then Governor George Wallace's infamous "stand in the schoolhouse door." In 2010, the campus saw the construction of the Malone-Hood Plaza and Autherine Lucy Clock Tower (the latter named for the first black student actually to enroll at UA in 1956, who stayed only three days before her safety was officially deemed to be under threat and she was expelled). These memorials came on the heels of renovating the auditorium where students once enrolled in classes – a process that was not at all a sure thing, the building having fallen into disrepair for some time.

A few elements stuck out to me about the 2010 dedication of the renovated Foster Auditorium and the new plaza/clock tower. The day's events were, of course, pitched as being about the significance of students Vivian Malone and James Hood and about the sequence of events at Foster of June 11, 1963. Rhetoric in the program booklet extended broad praise to the courage and tenacity of Malone and Hood; however, it became evident pretty quickly that the ceremonial events had far more to do with the University today. Those of us in attendance heard much about the "commitment to diversity" the institution now maintains, the inspiration drawn from figures like Malone and Hood, and the multitude of opportunities available to students today.

Conspicuously absent from the commemoration was any substantive mention of the attitudes about racial integration on campus at the time, or of the consistent threat of violence then aimed at African Americans in the community. There was little mention of "race" at all, in fact. Instead, those in attendance were asked to think broadly about the enduring power of "the human spirit" and to celebrate the resolve of determined individuals. The dedication of the new plaza was – as suggested by an accompanying website that contains video footage from the commemoration, descriptions of the major players in desegregating the University, and a timeline of events – about "A New Beginning: A Tribute to Courage and Progress."

Some people, myself included, were frustrated with what we deemed to be a literal whitewashing of a very complicated day and series of events leading to integration at UA. We constituted a group of (as we saw it) forward-thinking professors, several of us with specialties in African American studies. But in our follow-up to the commemoration – we organized roundtable discussions and various events on the topic of African American history at the University – there was an attempt to get the story *right* and to tell people what *really* happened. Thus, the focus of many responses to the plaza and clock tower dedication was its own specific and exacting narrative, one that attempted to "recuperate" what interested parties were convinced "really" happened in 1963.

Therein lies my own interest, as well as what I think is useful to think about vis-à-vis broader studies of identity and the oft-deployed notion of "cultural memory" (a fly in my intellectual soup, I'll admit). Namely, I would argue that commemoration is like any other mode of exegesis. That is, we think we can approach the past as a stable thing that will hold still and reveal its mysteries and lessons to us if we are simply careful enough observers. The past becomes in this way a text whose meaning we think we can access and extract. How else can a day *"live* in infamy"?

Besides, the new narrative of what "really" took place during the events leading up to UA's desegregation was choosy in its own telling, too, leaving out what might have run counter to its mission. What many of my fellow faculty did not talk about, for instance, were Autherine Lucy's words when she took to the podium at the commemoration ceremony. Far from insisting on an institutional comeuppance, she was full of gratitude for all that she considered the University to have done for her, beginning her brief comments by asking, in fact, if she were in heaven. James Hood gave his own short address, emphasizing his interest not in being a Civil Rights pioneer but instead in simply going to class. The very people whose histories were at play in the rhetorical tug-of-war between administrators and those who wanted to present a truer, unedited narrative did not exactly follow the script we progressively-minded race scholars wanted. When the voices scholars try to recuperate disagree with their advocates, what are we to make of it?

The point is not *not* to commemorate, necessarily (unless you're interested in avoiding those pesky party hats altogether, which is fair enough, though it probably won't make you popular at family gatherings). I see the issue instead as being one of recognizing that commemoration is inevitably about people making choices on how to commemorate. It's a matter of keeping our eyes on the ball. And in this case, the ball isn't Foster Auditorium or desegregation. It's a campus (well, more specifically, an administration or planning committee) navigating ways to talk about its more embarrassing moments.

K. Merinda Simmons is an Associate Professor in the Department of Religious Studies at the University of Alabama. Her research and writing are primarily concerned with the ways in which authenticity claims appear in theories of gender and race.

We Are What We Archive

Elonda Clay

Somedays I get stuck. Stuck wondering, "Where the hell did this thing come from?" There are wonderful old pictures of unknown people from years gone by or hotels that have long since seen their demise. I spend at least an hour a day rummaging through the storage area with Dictaphones tucked away in corner shelves, framed portraits of once distinguished college administrators, medals of honor once worn by Tuskegee airmen, and college records that, having outlived their usefulness, all find quiet retirement in acid-free corrugated boxes. I've even found photographs of an unsuspecting past president during the time he was governor of a state called Arkansas. Archives, as the keepers of all things old, are chock-full of images, photos, music, and stories, the stuff of which dreams of a past – and who we are in the present – are made.

So, as an archivist, the question of origins is a question that I wrestle with daily. People come to me wanting to know, When was this picture of the Liberty Parade in downtown Little Rock taken? Are the founding members of my fraternity's chapter in the 1942 college yearbook? Who is this in the 1960 Little Rock Sit-Ins picture? Where was Budlong Hall and who was Budlong anyway? Often, the only reply I have to offer is an unsettling "I don't know." But I have learned to creatively say "I don't know" in a myriad of ways, using words like "unidentified child," "picture taken circa 1870s," "miscellaneous items," "catalogs (some missing)," and "donor unknown." This daily process of micro-level origins construction, identification, and filling in the inevitable gaps in the record (with a lot of the work being done by the "c." that abbreviates the Latin "circa" [meaning approximately, about, maybe even round about...]) is a subtle, almost automatic activity for me – as it may likely be for anyone looking at an old family album, not sure who that person in the back of the photo is..., or was... – if only because I hate to see archives patrons, on an origins quest of their own, leave empty-handed.

The making of an archive, what Michel-Rolph Trouillot describes (in *Silencing the Past: Power and the Production of History* [1995]) as the moment of fact assembly in the process of producing history, is very much about valuing some artifacts over others, collecting these books instead of those books, preserving photos of famous or familiar people over ordinary

people, and saving only the records of specific institutions or organizations. The archive itself constitutes an assemblage of sorts – with config-
urations of materials, monographs, ideas, politics, people, and happenings
– and these relations are malleably aligned with power and the production
or making of historical narratives. For Trouillot, mentions and silences
are active practices; they are neither neutral nor natural. I've been trained
to make sure patrons have something, anything, from the archive to use
for the (re)creation of their personal or a wider institutional identity, for
their strategies of historicizing, or for their origin-tellings..., um, I mean
narratives. For origin-tellings, especially those timelines that combine first
founders, building cornerstones, initial meetings, or surprising successes,
claim to give us access to the germinating seeds that have spawned great
social movements or even our current historical moment. And yet, even
origin-tellings are often contested narratives of people, things, and events
that we inherit as well as observe; offering us at best a parallax view of
multiple pasts.

For instance, Simmons's essay reminds us that for every commemoration there are multiple strategies of (re)presentation and articulation that
reveal as much as they conceal. In the United States, for example, strategies
for telling the stories of desegregation, the Civil Rights movement, and the
current legacies of both often bifurcate along racial lines. Historian David
Blight, in his book *Race and Reunion* (2001), suggests that contending
memories of American history often clash and intermingle in public
memory; however, race often functions as a central pivot in determining
how Americans make choices to remember and forget the various details
of American history and politics. While tropes of progress toward racial
equality since desegregation are overused to the point of becoming cliché,
there is something about the claims, silences, and counterclaims of "coming
such a mighty long way," made by competing social interests and actors,
that smudges and maybe even cracks the pristine rear-view mirror of how
many of us today talk about racial integration back then.

These differences in how we remember and commemorate desegregation pique my curiosity. What are we to make of them? What is at stake
in these differences? For example, unlike the commemoration ceremony at
the University of Alabama celebrating desegregation that barely mentioned
race (as Simmons describes it), race (as a marker of collective group identification and distinction) is given a special place of honor at many ceremonies
at HBCUs (i.e., historically black colleges and universities) throughout
the US. For example, many HBCUs commemorate desegregation through
events connected with narratives of the significance of racial identity in the

struggle for Civil Rights. During a recent event commemorating the fiftieth anniversary of the 1964 Civil Rights Act, emphasis was placed on the role HBCU students played in fighting segregation through sit-ins and boycotts during the late 1950s–60s. These alternative desegregation stories were then often tied to contemporary conditions that confirm the persistence of segregation, racial tensions, racial inequality, and the exploitation and commercialization of Civil Rights history; hardly the victorious "triumph of diversity" rhetoric used in the University of Alabama commemoration.

This suggests that what ends up getting commemorated and what ends up fading from memory depends not on the key moments in an institution's racial integration timeline, but rather on who is telling the story of how legal racial segregation ended, and thus on how they choose to reassemble the story's details, where they fill in the gaps and with what. Where I work, Philander Smith College (a four-year HBCU located in Little Rock, Arkansas), prevalent claims concerning racial progress are not related to diversity or integration per se but, rather, to the enduring residual struggle for racial equality, the accomplishments of educated, exceptional bourgeois blacks, and, of course, the "uplifting of the race." In fact, the college's motto, "Think Justice," reflects not only a mission statement of academics in support of social justice, but also a rhetoric that repeats the very reason Philander Smith came into existence in the first place: to address post-Emancipation injustices related to black freed persons, which included limited higher education opportunities. So it is understandable that Philander Smith's current strategies of selecting from the archives and narrativizing its past are rarely of the whitewashing variety, at least as deployed during the University of Alabama's commemoration of desegregation; rather, I would describe them as doing the exact opposite: silencing or obscuring a white past. Lost are the overly-nostalgic rear-view mirrors of once generous whites as heroic figures in suffering blacks' struggle for higher education.

Now, I am keenly aware that, in my role as archivist to the college, the community and racial politics informing my own strategies of remembering and silencing the history of Philander Smith College as well as Philander Smith's place in Arkansas and American History are hardly naïve. I, like Simmons and her fellow band of professor/dissenters, consider my work to be that of disrupting normative frames of historical reference, doing so by revisiting the past to extract what could be called a subversive or insurgent history of desegregation.

I'll use the wall displays in the Archives Reading Room as an example. I have not placed any pictures of the college's founding father here. Although the room does have story boards on the timeline of the college's development, the majority of the walls are filled with portraits of the college's thirteen presidents, successful PSC graduates (such as United States Surgeon General Joycelyn Elders), books on black sports heroes before integration, and speakers from our social justice lecture series, Bless The Mic. For most of the college's students today, Philander Smith was simply some old white Civil War dude that the school happens to be named after. I do nothing in the Archives' visual space to change that, instead aiming to achieve the careful remembering and necessary forgetting to picture (and pitch) possible pasts to researchers and students. I like how James Baldwin puts it when he says, "history…does not refer merely, or even principally, to the past…. [I]t is to history that we owe our frames of reference, our identities, and our aspirations" (1966).

So somewhere between Philander Smith College's heroic commemoration of black college students' participation in Little Rock's early 1960s sit-ins and the University of Alabama's commemoration ceremony for Malone, Hood, and Lucy as honored diversity pioneers lies the tug and push of origins and identifications, of remembering and forgetting, or giving voice and silencing – activities all routinely carried out today, by means of sorting through the archives and choosing how to best fill in the gaps. As Simmons has observed, our packaging of the past says more about the people remembering in the present than it says about the past being remembered.

Elonda Clay is the Digital Services Librarian/Archivist at Philander Smith College in Little Rock, Arkansas. She is also a doctoral student in Theology and Religious Studies at VU University of Amsterdam, Netherlands. Her research interests include DNA ancestry testing and origins, religion and hip hop, and religion and the internet.

6. Constructing and Contesting the Nation

Patricide and the Nation

Steven Ramey

On June 15, 2013, violent attacks in the Pakistani province of Balochistan included a form of symbolic patricide, as a group fired rockets in the hill town of Ziarat to destroy a residence where Muhammad Ali Jinnah, regarded as the father of Pakistan, had stayed while recovering from an illness in 1948. The police officer guarding the site was killed in the attack. The same day saw other attacks in Balochistan that reportedly killed dozens, including bombings at a women's university and a hospital, both in the capital city of Quetta (a few hours away from Ziarat). While Lashkar-e-Jhangvi, which some people link with al Qaeda, claimed responsibility for the hospital and university attacks in Quetta, the Balochistan Liberation Army (BLA), identified as a separatist group trying to gain the independence of Balochistan from Pakistan, claimed the attack on Jinnah's residence.

Ironically, the next day was Father's Day in the United States, a manufactured holiday (like any other). Much like the promotion of socially-sanctioned sentiments through the mass production of "World's Greatest Dad" cards and mugs, the concept of nation and the unity that it implies requires the construction of an origins tale and the protection of both tangible and abstract symbols that represent that tale to generate the appropriate sentiments toward the nation and its unity. That separatists who reject the existence of the nation of Pakistan chose to attack a tangible element associated with the father of the nation is not coincidental. The greater focus in the media and among officials on the destruction of Jinnah's one-time residence, despite the larger number of lives lost in the other attacks, reflects the importance of such symbols. Some government officials in Balochistan expressly promised to restore Jinnah's residence in three or four months.

The broader context of the creation of Pakistan in 1947, dividing British India and related territories into two new nation-states, India and Pakistan, heightens the need for symbols that represent Jinnah's physical ties to the territory of the nation. Though he was born in Karachi, Pakistan, Jinnah, like millions of others who migrated in response to the Partition of British India, spent much of his adult life in what became India, specifically working as a lawyer in Bombay. This detail makes this site in Balochistan and stories of his childhood in Karachi, Pakistan, even more important in order to maintain the conception of a cohesive nation. The attacks on the same day in Quetta also reveal, in a more subtle fashion, the contested nature of that nation, as the attackers presumably targeted the Hazara people, an ethnic minority in Pakistan who generally identify as Shia Muslims. Organizations like Lashkar-e-Jhangvi consider the Hazara to be impure and thus not true members of the nation.

The official response to the assassination of Mohandas K. Gandhi in 1948 suggests a similar concern. Seen as the father of the Indian nation, Gandhi was both an important political leader and a symbol of the nation. After Nathuram Godse shot Gandhi, not only were he and his accused conspirators tried and two of them hanged, but the government also temporarily banned the Rashtriya Swayamsevak Sangh (RSS), an organization promoting a particular understanding of India as a Hindu nation, because of its alleged links to Godse and thus to Gandhi's assassination. Politicians in India sometimes still raise the assassination of Gandhi to denounce an opponent's ideology as out of bounds and dangerous. In February 2014, a Congress Party official associated the Bharatiya Janata Party (BJP) candidate for Prime Minister in an upcoming election with the RSS ideology that "killed Gandhi," to which partisans for the BJP responded that it had been the Congress Party's ideology that actually killed Gandhi.

Thus, the fathers of each nation, seen as central to the modern origins stories that facilitate the nations' construction, remain important symbols receiving significant attention. Physical symbols and holidays dedicated to them, as well as political rhetoric, all produce sentiments that help to maintain the nation-state and to promote particular political positions. Not everyone among the "children" of the national father, despite the efforts to produce those sentiments, accepts the reverence of the father or even the existence of the nation, making the symbol of the father of the nation also a target for attack. National holidays and monuments succeed when they generate positive sentiments about founders and the national identity, much as Father's Day reminds those of us who observe it to express (or sometimes generates in us) love and appreciation for our fathers (who are part of our personal origins stories), even if we do so in trite, exaggerated ways.

Steven Ramey is Associate Professor in the Department of Religious Studies and Director of Asian Studies at the University of Alabama. His research has focused on the contested nature of identities in contemporary India and elsewhere.

Our Disparate Fathers

Alexis Glenn

In "Patricide and the Nation," Steven Ramey constructs a distinct argument concerning the role and function of symbolic "father figures" and symbolic patricide within the founding context of modern India and Pakistan. Such figures are taken to occupy integral positions within national origins tales and are generative of particular sentiments within the national constituent body. The protection and promotion of such multivalent symbolic figures, Ramey argues, is required to maintain the conceptual integrity of the nation "and the unity that it implies." Disruptive political crises "heighten the need" for such symbols, Ramey urges, because of their assumed unitive capacity and their ability to cultivate particular public sentiments in the interest of national solidarity.

It is against this general formulation of symbolic national unity that I will argue; for symbolic patricide and related episodes of political violence suggest critical disagreement between parties regarding the content and meaning of such symbolic figures, as well as their position and function within a national origins tale. Instances of symbolic patricide, I contend, do not constitute an ideological conflict over a singular, unified concept of the nation, but are, instead, representative of divergent understandings among individuals and between parties within "the nation." Rather than sites of conceptual unity, the symbolic father figures described by Ramey may be alternatively analyzed as sites of conceptual conflict, figures whose emotionally generative capacity and orientation within an origins tale are continuously contested and renegotiated.

Symbolic conflict within "Patricide and the Nation" may be discerned on two general levels: that of national "father figures" and the public sentiments which they generate, and that of the concept of "the nation" as such. The contested nature of symbolic father figures may be detected in the violent actions taken against themselves or their representative elements, as in the case of the bombing of Muhammad Ali Jinnah's former residence. While it may be argued that Jinnah, regarded as the father of modern Pakistan, occupies a central role within Pakistan's origins tale, it is by no means clear that his role is similarly perceived as "unifying" across the national constituent body. This point becomes evident when one considers the party responsible for the bombing of his residence, the Balochistan

Liberation Army (BLA). Ramey maintains that the separatists chose to attack a tangible symbol associated with Jinnah due to their fundamental rejection of the existence of Pakistan as one nation. He appears to claim that an outright rejection by separatists of Jinnah's legitimacy within Pakistan's origins tale does not threaten the conceptual integrity of that tale for non-separatists. One may question, however, whether this violent act stemmed from outright rejection or, rather, from the contested symbolic nature of Jinnah himself.

It could be argued that the BLA did not necessarily "reject" Jinnah or the existence of the Pakistani nation, but rather sought to renegotiate his position within a different national origins tale through violent means. In this interpretation, symbolic representations of Jinnah and the Pakistani nation itself maintain an important position within the origins tales told by separatists and non-separatists alike, but are conceived as sites of ongoing contestation and disunity rather than unitive loci around which origins tales are organized and nations are constructed. After all, if separatists completely rejected Jinnah's political and symbolic importance, there would be no conceivable reason to attack a tangible symbol associated with his memory. Such rejected representations arguably become politically impotent, stripping them of authoritative power and symbolic purpose. So perhaps the attack on Jinnah's residence was not evidence of his rejection by the BLA, but rather of their attempt to renegotiate the symbolic position of a contested "father figure" within their own divergent origins tale. One may then conceive of Jinnah himself not as a symbolic representation of national unity, but, instead, as a symbolic site of ideological confrontation and political dissension with respect to his relative position within different national origins tales.

This logic may be extended to Ramey's treatment of the official state response to Mohandas K. Gandhi's assassination. Set against claims of national unity and symbolic cohesion, the contested status of Gandhi as father of the Indian nation may be discerned not only from the assassination itself, but also in the suppressive response of the Indian state against the offenders. As a "symbol of the [Indian] nation," Ramey contends that the unified national legacy associated with Gandhi must often be protected against those opponents whose ideology is characterized as "out of bounds and dangerous." Such ideological commitments imbued the politico-religious group responsible for the assassination, the Rashtriya Swayamsevak Sangh (RSS), which actively promoted conceptualizations of India divergent from official state narratives. While it may be generally argued that Gandhi, like Jinnah, occupies a position of importance within Indian origins tales, the fact of his assassination and the subsequent punitive state response seem to imply violent conditions of political contestation surrounding his symbolic status, rather than a cohesive national unity in need of protection from ideological interlopers. Indeed, these facts suggest the existence of multiple competing origins tales altogether, of which the official state-sponsored origins narrative is merely one.

In the context of appeals to symbolic unity and cohesive national identity, such "father figures" must be understood as symbolic sites of conceptual conflict with respect to the modern nation-state, whose relative position within a particular origins tale and ability to generate particular sentiments among citizens are continuously contested and reformulated. While Ramey briefly mentions incidents of violent contestation within Pakistan and India concerning the symbolic status of such figures, these arguments are displaced by those privileging general cohesion across parties to a unified national ideal. The phenomenon of symbolic patricide itself, besides the ancillary moments of violent political disputation, indicates conditions of vital discord between citizens regarding the relative symbolic authority of such "father figures," as well as their orientation within divergent national origins tales.

I have contended that cases of symbolic patricide are representative of acutely disparate conceptualizations of "the nation" as such, rather than instances of ideological competition over an objective concept of symbolic national unity. Interpreting episodes of symbolic patricide in this way not only serves to represent in an historically accurate manner the complexity of the practical and ideological roles of such "father figures" (as viewed by citizens and political parties), but also creates discursive space for the competitive interplay of divergent articulations and embodiments of "the nation" itself.

Alexis Glenn is a PhD candidate in Religious Studies at Brown University, Providence, specializing in the subfield of Religion and Critical Thought, focusing primarily on political theory, virtue ethics, and early modern Anglo-American history.

7. Knowing When Not to Laugh

Searching for Chimaeras

Vaia Touna

In the summer of 2013 while I was hosting Andie Alexander for a week or so in Thessaloniki, Greece, I decided that among our day trips should be a visit to Mount Olympus (a destination that is, I know, among the highlights of any visit to Greece – that and the Parthenon in Athens, of course). So one day we took the highway south, toward Athens. After about a two-hour drive from Thessaloniki we reached the slopes of the mountain, which myth has it was the home of the "Twelve Gods" of the ancient Greeks. Over bumpy roads and narrow passages that made for a thrilling experience, we drove up the mountain to a shelter (a youth hostel with coffee service), which was at 1,000 meters above sea level, or about 2,000 meters below the top of the mountain top, surrounded by thick vegetation and with a wonderful view of the Aegean Sea and the Gulf of Thessaloniki.

We ordered our frappés (a foamed-covered iced coffee which is considered by many a national drink – it was, after all, invented by a Greek!) and soon found ourselves in the middle of a conversation with the owner of the shelter, along with a couple, who, like us, had come to spend the day in this idyllic spot. It was a conversation about how the ongoing economic crisis had affected his business (a common theme in Greece these days, like talking about the weather elsewhere), and as one question led to the other, we learned that the people who visited his shelter (apart from Greeks, that is), were mostly Russians and Germans. This prompted me to ask him if he knew why these tourists were visiting Mount Olympus – apart, that is, from being drawn to it simply because of the history and mythology that surrounds this mountain. With a wide, sardonic smile he told us that some of them were searching for the "actual" throne of Zeus. We all, of course, burst out laughing. Now, I should note that there is high on the mountain a location that is actually named "The Throne of Zeus," or Stefani, and for all we know that's where these people wanted to go. However, the point here is not so much the actual intentions of those tourists but, rather, the assumption of the owner of the hostel and, of course, our reaction upon hearing his story. A few days later I ran across this site: http://www.parallaximag.gr/thessaloniki/o-kipos-ton-anamniseon. It talked about the recasting of a public space in Thessaloniki that was turned into a park, and described it as follows:

> The garden after the renovation was named "Garden of Memories" as it contains elements of the gardening techniques of Thessaloniki during the ancient, Byzantine, and Roman periods.

That the author of the post was so certain about the kind of gardening techniques actually used 2,000 years ago, and which are obviously in use today, led me to recall the tourists' quest for the throne of Zeus and our reaction when we heard about it. That we all search for chimaeras, and sometimes think we have found them, is obviously not news. All sorts of funding is available for searching for everything from, say, the "religious gene" to the meaning of texts that are thousands of years old and covered with multiple contexts and narratives, and even to discovering the lost Atlantis. What *is* of interest here, I think, is that these quests for origins don't make us burst into laughter (quite the contrary actually, for serious money supports such quests) as easily as, say, searching for the throne of Zeus, and this is something that I personally find very curious. That is, what – or rather *who* (and *how*, and *toward what ends*) – makes certain chimaeras more real than others and therefore worth pursuing? Answering that is my quest!

Vaia Touna is an Assistant Professor in the Department of Religious Studies at the University of Alabama. Her research focuses on the sociology of identity formation with examples drawn from ancient to modern Greece.

"A Joke's a Very Serious Thing"

Tara Baldrick-Morrone

In the fourth section in Book One of *The Gay Science*, Friedrich Nietzsche plays with the conventional understanding of "good" and "evil": that which is "good" is presented as the well-established customs and traditions of a given society, the "old boundary stones and pieties." In contrast, "evil" is associated with that which is "new, daring, unattempted." In this sense, "good" is "old" and all that is known, while "evil" is all that is contrary and "new." With this subversive connotation in mind, Nietzsche contends that within each subsequent generation of moral and religious leaders and teachers, one can find the same "mischief," namely, a desire to assert oneself and one's values over against the entrenched traditions of the day. Although Nietzsche does not make the move to say that the "evil" leaders and teachers prevail by masking the "new" as the "old," I want to push his playful manipulation of what we understand as "good" and "evil" into new territory. Doing so, I think, will help illustrate the work that discourses on origins do, for by representing a "new" position as familiar, commonplace, and "old," one is able to authorize a particular perspective as legitimate and authoritative.

As a student of late antiquity, I have grown increasingly aware of the way that the assertion of some *thing*'s antiquity, be it a text, an idea, or an artifact, serves to legitimate both the object in question and the social group with which it is affiliated. For example, in the New Testament, the Gospel of Matthew portrays the character of Jesus as often framing his "new" teachings in the idiom of rabbinic exegesis – that is, authorizing his point by providing a close reading of Jewish law – in order to show his opponents that his claims do not stand in contrast to the Torah. His interpretation is not meant to abolish the law but to fulfill it. By connecting his innovative interpretation with the "old" law, he thereby grounds his claims in the legitimacy of the shared, established traditions of his audience. Thus, the social group that he represents (a particular form of Jewish Christianity) becomes more legitimate and authoritative than other groups (in the case of the Matthean narrative, this would be the scribes and Pharisees).

It is important to recognize that this kind of rhetorical strategy is employed not only by various groups in the ancient world, but also by more contemporary social groups, such as the guild of scholars that we label "the academy." Several of the disciplines that scholars of religion use to analyze antiquity can largely be seen as a sort of quest for origins. Specific fields such as those concerning philology and textual studies that seek out the original readings of texts are often aimed at providing particular readings with greater weight over against other readings. This is, of course, not limited to scholars of antiquity or even religion, as these same types of inquiries are pursued in many different areas of study. Nor are these quests and associations with the past restricted to scholarship: quite often, these same discourses are used in the classroom.

Consider the way that certain "traditions" are approached in introductory courses. It is frequently the case that episodes of the TV series *South Park* are shown to students in order to introduce and illustrate the (fantastic) origins of "newer traditions" like "Mormonism" and "Scientology." I imagine that this is done uncritically much of the time, perhaps in an effort to dismiss such ideas. However, I would venture to guess that many would not even dare to show episodes that detail (equally fantastic) origins stories of "Judaism" or "Islam" as uncritically as they do for "newer traditions." This is not to say that one should be equally as reverent of Scientology's origins as one is of Judaism's – quite the contrary. My point is that we should be reverent of neither, for one's antiquity should not exempt it from critical study. Here, I come back to Nietzsche's point above, that oftentimes what are seen as the "old boundary stones" are uncritically taken as "good." I would go a step further to say that these more ancient "traditions" are even taken more seriously, for the mention of auditing with the help of a Hubbard Electropsychometer would perhaps elicit more incredulous expressions from both students and scholars alike than, say, transubstantiation (the idea that some bread and wine turns into a dead man's actual body and blood).

In his oft-cited "Theses on Method," Bruce Lincoln (1996) advocates for a relentless pursuit of the temporal and contingent dimensions of discourses – such as those found in our objects of study and even in our peers' scholarship and thinking. As he argues, the following questions should be at the center of our inquiries:

Who speaks here?
To what audience? In what immediate and broader context? Through what system of mediations? With what interests?...
Of what would the speaker(s) persuade the audience? What are the consequences if this project of persuasion should happen to succeed? Who wins what, and how much? Who, conversely, loses?

By asking such questions, we can then begin to answer just why it is that certain lines of scholarly investigations are treated as more important, more legitimate, and more worthwhile than others. So perhaps, instead of asking which of these quests and discourses make us "burst into laughter" or which chimaeras are considered more "real," it would indeed be more fruitful, I think, to ask why certain subjects are treated with more sincerity or even "reverence" than others. In our own scholarly pursuits, then, it is important to remain ever-mindful neither to uncritically reproduce the discourses of the groups that we study nor to flippantly dismiss those discourses as unworthy of critique.

Tara Baldrick-Morrone is a PhD candidate specializing in religions of western antiquity in the Department of Religion at Florida State University. Her research focuses on rhetoric and conceptions of the body in late antiquity, as well as issues of theory and pedagogy in the introductory classroom.

8. The Good Old Days

The Way We Were...?

K. Merinda Simmons

I've always been fascinated by those birthday cards that offer a little person-alized nostalgia for yesteryear to our elderly loved ones who are able to tell us stories about "back in the day when...." I'm talking specifically about the cards that you typically see in gas stations and Cracker Barrels, the ones that try to give a societal snapshot from the day someone was born. They remind my father (born in 1942), for example, that the hit single on the day of his birth was Bing Crosby's "White Christmas" (it had recently overtaken "[I've Got a Gal in] Kalamazoo") and that gas back then cost only 19 cents a gallon. For that matter, the 19-cent gas would have fuelled a new car that someone could buy for just over a thousand bucks. And so on.

Every time, it was always the same: when on car journeys to visit the extended family we would stop for gas or for some Southern eats on the highways between our respective cities, I would make my way through the displays of porcelain chicken cookie jars and decorative aprons to the racks of these cards, eager to read how the world looked on some random day in 1954.

I wish I could say I was filing through them with a sense of irony, rolling my eyes at how silly it is to think that any snapshot says something about anything other than the person taking the proverbial picture. I'm a savvy theorist, after all! I eat hokey additions to the nostalgia market for breakfast! Well, not really...I prefer an Uncle Herschel's Special. And I wasn't reading those cards with any sense of irony.

Cut to: My car, a couple of years back – I'm on my way to campus one morning, listening to Alabama Public Radio (APR). Suddenly I hear the dulcet, lip-smacking voice of the late Kathryn Tucker Windham (b. 1918). A local celebrity of sorts, she made a name for herself as she went from small-town journalist to Alabamian storyteller, ultimately living to the ripe old age of 93. She had a series for some time on APR, offering weekly "stories" (later called "commentaries," presumably when the production team caught wind of the fact that there was no narrative arc) every Friday morning. I enjoyed listening to her – there was something about the sing-songy cadence of her distractable musings. Inevitably, the soft punchline of every story was always something to the effect of things just not being the way they used to be. Her memories reflected her hankering for the "good old days" of "simpler times."

One that stands out is her bit, "Old Sayings Forgotten," wherein she describes her love of the colloquialisms that surrounded her as a child. When responding to someone who asked after her when she was ill, she found herself tossing out what her father used to say: "I couldn't holler 'sooey' if the hogs had me." This gets her thinking about what she considers to be the unfortunate evolution into the digital age that has taken away "colorful expressions" and replaced them with a generation that doesn't know how to have a conversation. She reminisces about sayings like "mad as a settin' hen," going on to wistfully bemoan the entrée of email. Her solution? Someone should make a long list of old expressions so that people can start incorporating them into everyday parlance again.

No wonder she was so popular, right? Folks could longingly meander down memory lane with her, or, in the case of us non-Alabamian natives – us academic emigrants from other locales – we could congratulate ourselves on our appreciation of a quaint folk scene and fancy ourselves embedded in a charming brand of Southern culture (while, of course, reserving the right to distance ourselves from the same at academic conferences).

Of course, with the praise of how things were done "back in the day," comes a critique of contemporary society – in the instance of the bit above, a disdain for what she sees as the pseudo-communication of emailing, a lack of conversations in general in this technological era, and thus the fear of extinction of a mode of discourse she finds more authentic.

There's no denying it: nostalgia sells. And despite all my disclaimers, I don't mind admitting that I'm an occasional customer. What's important to…hey, *remember!*…is that a look backward in time, while pleasant to indulge in among nears and dears, does not *preserve* some pristine portrait of the way things were any more than do those Cracker Barrel cards. Students in my seminar on Religion in the American South talk about this approach to talking about the past vis-à-vis Scarlett O'Hara and the way that figurines of the character are still sold for lots of money as collectibles to people interested in antiques. There is no Scarlett O'Hara, after all – not with her dresses and classic 17-inch waist – without Mammy standing behind her lacing her corset. What we collect is not Scarlett O'Hara *herself* but rather a product of a specific moment in time, made possible by a complex web of domestic servitude, ideas about Southern femininity, and plantation societies.

How much "simpler" a certain time was depends, then, on who's talking, on the person for whom it was simpler. Andy Griffith's Mayberry, like Kathryn Tucker Windham's Alabama, might have been a simple place of good biscuits and sapling fishing poles for some of its inhabitants, but between Jim Crow and gender discrimination (as just two quick examples), there are plenty of people for whom those years were not what one might call the good old days.

In the segment "Even Better Than the Real Thing," *The Daily Show* gets at this idea with correspondent John Oliver's quest, predicated by conservative voices calling for a return to the values of an America in which they grew up, for a so-called simpler time in history. First he talks to the executive behind the famous "Coke and a smile" ad campaign of the 1970s invoked by Glenn Beck as an example of this better America, only to be reminded in the interview about the unending gas lines and the Iranian Revolution that both occurred in the same decade. He goes back further, but the '60s held big problems where rights for women and African Americans were concerned. The piece continues like this, as Oliver gathers reflections about the '50s, '40s, and '30s, each time hearing about the hardships in each decade. He finally arrives at a conclusion. The pundits who long for a simpler era summon their examples with, "When I was a kid...." Oliver's eureka moment comes with his realization that the commentators remember times being uncomplicated and happy because they were children – *of course* things were simpler!

Anxieties over whether small-town culture or a certain way of life has been "lost" presume that there was an actual thing to lose in the first place. And if we're really looking for things to be simple, it seems like there'd be something simpler in just admitting that simplicity is an idea of our own making.

K. Merinda Simmons is an Associate Professor in the Department of Religious Studies at the University of Alabama. Her research and writing are primarily concerned with the ways in which authenticity claims appear in theories of gender and race.

The Way We Worked...

James Dennis LoRusso

In 1996, TriStar Pictures released *Jerry Maguire*, in which the hero of the same name (played by Tom Cruise) faces a mid-life crisis, leaving a promising career as a sports agent to seek fulfillment in a simpler life. He yearns to return to the "simpler pleasures of the job," to a time when people mattered more than profits. Nostalgia, then, is an essential plot device, offering audiences a vivid picture of "the way we worked." Merinda Simmons, in her essay, suggests that such appeals to "simpler times" say more about the present than our past. They provide us with an epic past, an orientation point from which we can make sense of our contemporary experiences. As I shall argue, the nostalgic views about "work" in *Jerry Maguire* are nothing new, but rather part of a much longer tradition of reimagining the meaning of "work" in American popular culture, evident particularly in Arthur Miller's play, *Death of a Salesman*. This nostalgia reveals less about the way people actually labored in the past and more about how American popular culture wrestles with the complexities of daily life.

Jerry Maguire offers its audience a glimpse into a lost world through Jerry's periodic flashbacks to his mentor and founder of Sports Management International (SMI), Dicky Fox (played by Jared Jussim). These brief scenes feature a middle-aged Fox sitting behind his desk in an office that looks remarkably antiquated in relation to the sleek aesthetic of Maguire's workplace in the film's present. Wholly absent are the desktops, laptops, cellphones, and other technical marvels of late twentieth-century life, devices that that dominate the rest of the film. Other than a few files, some stacks of paperwork, and an unassuming nameplate on a wooden desk, Fox's office is austere, in contrast to the chaotic mire of scattered papers, multiple computer terminals, dartboards, and athletic posters that adorn Maguire's workspace.

The juxtaposition of these two images produces a moral claim regarding the character of modern work. "Back in the day," work was orderly, predictable, and strictly demarcated from leisure, unlike the workplace of "today," which technology has rendered unmanageable, where the rapid pace imposes longer hours, increased workload, and the need for employees to bring their leisure to the job. Without making the claim explicit, *Jerry*

Maguire clearly prefers the era of Dicky Fox, a time before the corrosive effects of financial success and corporate growth had inevitably altered everything. The sagacious Dicky Fox provides audiences with a vision of a simpler life grounded in a particular conception of "work." Foremost, he reminds us that work is fundamentally a reflection of the inner disposition of the individual, declaring, "If this [placing his hand on his heart] is empty, this [pointing to his head] doesn't matter." A job requires more than intelligence, more than one's rational faculties; when Fox says "the key to this business is personal relationships," he suggests that a job demands the involvement of the whole person: mind, body, and "soul," and of these, the last is most essential.

In fact, the film opens with Jerry's "breakthrough," a kind of "dark night of the soul," in which he realizes that his life, in particular his job, has taken a wrong turn. He is compelled to write a "mission statement" calling for "fewer clients, less money, more attention." Jerry confesses:

> Suddenly, I was my father's son again. I was remembering the simple pleasures of the job, how I ended up here out of law school, the way a stadium sounds when one of my players performs well on the field. The way we are meant to protect them in health and in injury. With so many clients, we had forgotten what was important.

The nostalgia of simpler times therefore lays the foundation for his critique of the business. He becomes "his father's son" and recalls a lost innocence that had driven him to pursue a career as a sports agent. Not money or power, but the "simple pleasures" of the game and compassion for the players were what mattered. In short, work should be meaningful, as it once had been.

The scene culminates with Maguire boldly declaring: "I was thirty-five. I had started my life." The film, from its beginning, then, frames the story as a redemption narrative, of a man who comes to understand that his work cannot merely be a means to prestige or material prosperity, but ultimately should represent an opportunity to actualize certain principles, to serve as an expression of his humanity. Likewise, as a piece of popular culture, *Jerry Maguire* actively beckons its audience to awaken to this revelation. It instructs the viewer in the moral claim that work should transcend material rewards, that it should possess us as intrinsically valuable and facilitate our highest ideals.

The scenes with Dicky Fox exhibit a timelessness that proves difficult to pinpoint. The lack of technology and his generic business attire conceal any clue about the specific historical period in which they take place. Yet, if Jerry is in his mid-thirties in 1996, when the movie was released, then the flashbacks to Dicky Fox could not be more than a decade earlier. The passage above tells us he first completed law school before working at SMI, which means that he was likely in his early twenties at the time. It is a safe assumption, therefore, that the "simpler times" that so appeal to Maguire occur sometime during the early to mid-1980s, a period in American capitalism often remembered for terms like "mergers and acquisitions," "hostile takeovers," and "downsizing." Certainly, for many Americans, these were anything but idyllic, simple times.

As Simmons reminds us, "How much 'simpler' a certain time was depends, then, on who's talking." For Maguire, the earlier time may have been simpler, but his nostalgia overlooks the complicated social processes and structures that enable the portrait of Dicky Fox to exist in the first place. Rather than a reflection of simpler times, sports agencies emerged as product of the increasing specialization and complexity in the sports "industry." Maguire's selective memories of Dicky Fox, then, point not to some pristine past, but rather to a particularly powerful ideology of work in the American cultural imaginary.

Nearly fifty years before *Jerry Maguire*, for instance, Arthur Miller makes use of a similar rhetoric about work to levy a critique against society in *Death of a Salesman* (1949). The protagonist, Willy Loman, an ageing salesman living in Brooklyn, yearns for a return to a simpler time when people mattered in the sales industry. In a pivotal scene (Act 2, Scene 2), Loman credits one man, a salesman named Dave Singleton who worked till he was eighty-four, with helping him realize that "selling was the greatest career a man could want." Loman idolizes the personal connection that selling seemed to afford Singleton. He "could go, at the age of eighty-four, into twenty or thirty different cities, and pick up the phone, and be remembered and loved and helped by so many different people."

Like Maguire's memory of Dicky Fox, the image of Dave Singleton here contrasts starkly with the dismal realities of Loman's own life. He represents "the way we were," when the work of a salesman bestowed intrinsic rewards. Just prior to losing his job, Loman castigates his boss:

> In those days there was personality in it, Howard. There was respect, and comradeship, and gratitude in it. Today, it's all cut and dried, and there's no chance for bringing friendship to bear – or personality. You see what I mean? They don't know me anymore.

Here, we see the same desire in Willy for the "personal" that Maguire seeks. He, too, covets work that facilitates a human connection and respects the dignity of each individual, to know others and to be known. Clearly, then, this sense that work has lost something of its true nature is nothing unique to the late twentieth century. Separated by almost five decades, both Loman and Maguire utilize nostalgia to explain their present dissatisfaction.

Despite their similarities, however, *Death of a Salesman* and *Jerry Maguire* lead to dramatically different conclusions. Whereas the latter is a story of personal triumph, *Death of a Salesman* ends in tragedy, with Loman's suicide when he drives his car off the road on a lonely evening. And while both are explorations of "the American Dream" – that hard work should not only lead to material success but also to personal fulfillment – Miller's critique reveals this dream as illusory, a delusion that eats away at an individual's will to live. In the context of postwar America, the character of Willy Loman struggles against the rise of a society of mass consumption, in which what one has rather than what one does is emerging as the primary act of self-identification. In this case, clinging to the misconception that work should bestow significance proves fatal.

Released in the final years of the twentieth century, *Jerry Maguire* draws on nostalgia to uphold rather than resist this ideology of work. Jerry's realization that people should matter saves him. In a globalized economy governed by the norms of neoliberalism, the film teaches us to break out, to become an entrepreneur not merely in one's career but of one's inner self. In the end, the historical sense that something has been lost therefore proves less important than the purposes that such nostalgia serves. For, as Simmons aptly notes, "simplicity is an idea of our own making," and we can appeal to its rhetorical potential to maintain or contest our daily experiences.

James Dennis LoRusso is a Visiting Research Fellow in the Center for the Study of Religion at Princeton University. His research concerns the social construction of religion in post-industrial America, with a focus on the workplace as a site of subject formation.

9. A Little Ambiguity Goes a Long Way

Coloring Columbus

Leslie Dorrough Smith

I am the parent of three children, two of whom are elementary school-aged. As such, I have now twice been handed a line-drawn image of Christopher Columbus that they each have dutifully colored, which appears to be a requisite kindergarten activity at our local public school. Because of the historical evidence that details Columbus's systematic torture and murder of the peoples whose lands he colonized, I have always found this exercise something akin to coloring a picture of Saddam Hussein or some other such figure. Perhaps in recognition of the controversy surrounding Columbus and the celebration of a day in his honor, the publishers of the coloring page that my children received inserted a caption under his image that reads, "Christopher Columbus: What kind of person do you think he was?" It is interesting that the take-home pictures of George Washington, Abraham Lincoln, and Martin Luther King, Jr. that the children also received did not ask that (or any other) question.

Beyond asking children to color a picture of someone who could be described as a mass-murderer, there is another irony at play in asking the aforementioned question: the information about Columbus presented within the curriculum is hardly sufficient to even begin to digest the question. Outside of learning that familiar jingle ("In 1492, Columbus sailed the ocean blue…"), the children know little else about him besides the names of his ships and how he had something to do with the "discovery" of America. Based on this information alone, it's quite natural to presume that, under the usual educational circumstances, most children are very inadequately equipped to grapple with what "kind" of person he was.

My object in mentioning this is to highlight the manner in which the stories that we often tell about our nation's past and its relationship to our present identity are tales that must, by definition, be incomplete and only vaguely rendered. Why? To put it simply, some of our most powerful symbols must be intentionally ambiguous if they are to remain useful; they must embody a certain degree of flexibility to support a larger, ongoing narrative capable of adaptation to the diversity and complexity of society's shifts while also creating the appearance of unity. We cannot be too specific about what we mean when we reference Columbus, for specificity involves discussing historical details and personal attributes that I suspect few die-hard patriots would like to associate with their country. It also means that the more positive concepts often associated with Columbus Day (i.e., a generic tip of the hat to patriotism and great sales at the mall) become harder to justify.

Similarly, consider the experience that my second grader had this past September 11. He has not yet encountered any sort of formal treatment of 9/11 at school except for the annual moment of silence that occurs on that morning (the significance of which he almost certainly doesn't understand). On September 10, he was simply instructed to "celebrate our country by wearing red, white, and blue" the next day. He was a little unsure why he was doing this (beyond the fact that his teacher told him to), but indeed, he wore precisely that, explaining his clothing choice as something "for America."

Somewhat differently, my fourth grader received a more in-depth discussion of what transpired that day in 2001; it appears that in the state curriculum, fourth grade is the first time when 9/11 is transformed from a relatively random moment of patriotism to a civics lesson in its own right. While she was aware that people died, her knowledge of 9/11 was not particularly well-developed. So when she came home from school, she had a wealth of new information to share: some people from far away had flown planes into important buildings, many people had died, and they watched a film about some children whose school had been displaced in the recovery process. I asked her if she knew why 9/11 had happened – if that question had come up at all. Her response was that no one had either offered or answered the "why" question. She had come home eagerly hoping that I would answer it for her.

My sense is that, as in the case of Columbus, this same sort of powerful, symbolic vagueness was once again at work in the renderings of 9/11 that each of my children received that day. Of course, there is wisdom in selectively discussing certain topics with children if only to prevent them from being constantly fearful or confused. But for most Americans, 9/11 is nothing if not frightening, confusing, and complicated, and so this begs the question of the relevance of its presence in any discussion geared toward children. Some might say that it's impossible not to talk about it, as its cultural presence is unavoidable. But this is a difficult position to accept, since things like poverty can be just as frightening, confusing, and pervasive (and likely more directly impactful to most children than 9/11), and yet this is a topic that remains unspoken throughout most of their lives.

I suspect that the reason why stories like Columbus and 9/11 receive such attention in our children's educations isn't because of the particular importance of transmitting a discrete set of facts about the person or event. Rather, the symbols embedded in such narratives (of American goodness, ingenuity, and confidence; of patriotism, liberty, and sacrifice) have become so critical to our present self-understanding that our children literally cannot become "one of us" without reading themselves into that same story. These instances comprise important examples of amorphous, albeit tremendously powerful, symbols that can be manipulated to mean whatever a culture needs them to mean in order to render a desirable depiction of itself in the current political and social climate. The fact that Columbus's character is now called into some question (if only barely) may represent a fundamentally different reframing of the discussion surrounding him, but the imprecision with which we continue to tell his story guarantees that that we can engineer the narrative to mean whatever we need. If we take seriously that the manner in which we socialize children is a mere reflection of the values, concerns, and realities manufactured by the larger culture, then a coloring page and some color-coordinated clothing are far more than mere child's play.

Leslie Dorrough Smith is Assistant Professor of Religious Studies and Chair of the Women's and Gender Studies program at Avila University, Kansas City. Her current research examines the interplay between gender, sex, reproduction, and the politics of American evangelical groups.

Tracing the Visible and Invisible

Martha Smith Roberts

The image of Christopher Columbus that Leslie Smith's children were asked to color in celebration of Columbus Day frames the holiday as a "neutral" representation of an historical moment in the founding of a nation. Even adding to the caption, "What kind of person do you think he was?" does not scratch the surface, she notes, of the implications of this complicated history, a history that is condensed and polished into a generic "explorer" figure for students to color as they listen to a story of "discovery." Smith's discussion asks us to examine the representations of American history and identity that are presented as natural and neutral, especially those that we use to educate the next generation of Americans.

I wonder, then, if we can use this visual history lesson to think about the politics of representing American origins as a process of making visible and invisible. For example, let's consider another coloring book version of this "origin" moment. This second image comes from artist Jesse Stone's interpretation of Howard Zinn's classic work, *A People's History of the United States* (2003). Stone, an artist from Springfield, Missouri, created a series of children's coloring book pages based on Howard Zinn's work. (Stone met with Zinn at Missouri State in the early 2000s; he approved of her visual interpretation.) Here, Columbus stands in a similarly proud pose, and in the foreground native children line up to bring him their treasures. A pile of tiny severed arms lies on the ground as well, from those who have failed to meet their quota. Handless children cry and die in the background. The caption reads: "Rich people in the Old World gave Columbus money to bring back gold from the Arawaks. If they didn't have gold, the men cut off their hands! Columbus and his men even cut off the hands of little Arawak children!" Suddenly, a very different story emerges before us, in an image that would be considered too violent or inappropriate for a Columbus Day lesson at an elementary school.

This second version draws very different lines, of course. Just as Zinn's volume endeavors to present American history from alternative perspectives by including the stories that are left out of traditional accounts, the coloring book version draws an image of violent origins by including the Arawak. This visibility responds to Zinn's critique of absence: "When we read the history books given to children in the United States, it all starts with heroic adventure – there is no bloodshed – and Columbus Day is a celebration. Past the elementary and high schools, there are only occasional hints of something else" (2003: 7). For Zinn, there is a gap of knowledge perpetuated by the educational system; minority voices and experiences are silenced in favor of a hindsight reconstruction that glorifies the nation-state. Making violence visible is one way of shifting the power of the Columbus origins story. It attempts to draw attention to perpetrators and to hold them accountable for their actions.

As Smith's article makes clear, the Columbus story of American origins is more about the present than the past. The United States' history of violence – the one that scholars like Zinn want to reveal in their work – is an uncomfortable history at best, a destabilizing one at worst. For Zinn, the absence of minority voices in historical retellings is not an oversimplification reserved for elementary school children. His work combs through the texts of historians who have created eerily similar versions of American origins. Columbus's story is not simply denied or ignored; it is acknowledged, and then the conquest and murder are quietly accepted in the name of progress. Thus it would appear that the violence of our Columbian myth of origins is glossed over, sent to the background, or pushed away from the field of vision to allow the greater visibility of the "significant past" that can, through this very lack of specificity, reproduce a particular national identity.

The coloring book image is an apt representation of how "leaving out the details" in the Columbus origins story is actually a strategic moment of inclusion and exclusion. Smith recognizes that the black-and-white coloring page is not at all "blank." It is "incomplete and vaguely rendered." It utilizes a "powerful symbolic vagueness" that makes certain elements of the story visible and others invisible. When children are asked to color "inside of the lines," they are being asked to reproduce the dominant narrative represented by the visible boundaries of the "lines." What is at stake here is *invisibility* in terms of race, nation, and religion. Comparing these two images helps us to tease out the violence of "neutrality." When the Columbus story is celebrated only in terms of "discovery," the racialized, nationalist, and religious biases are affirmed; the violence recedes – it is rendered invisible.

Smith's notion of a "powerful symbolic vagueness" that maintains national identity seems to be indeed crucial to origins stories of discovery, destiny, and progress. The ambiguity and the incomplete nature of these tales create a flexibility of emphasis, a visibility of certain themes that relies on the invisibility of others. Invisible violence still lingers in the image that Smith describes; however, unlike the piles of severed hands from Arawak children, this violence is disconnected from the victims and attached instead to a mythic narrative of a "greater good." This origins story – violence in service of a greater good – is one that persists implicitly in the "neutral" Columbus coloring page, and it is the one that is told again and again to create "American" identity. Thus, violence is not completely deleted from the story (Columbus holds a sword in his hand); in fact, it is necessary that it be there implicitly, as a way to perpetuate the further use of just, moral, or essential violence for the survival of the nation.

But Columbus's discovery of the Americas is just one of many foundational origins stories that perpetuate a particular racialized, national, and religious worldview. Like the story of American discovery, the story of American diversity is one that sublimates violence and exclusion in service of the vague yet evocative narrative of the greater good. The principles of religious freedom and diversity create the narrative foundation for a country that sees itself as representative of "the many." In this origins story, the US is a place of refuge, a space where a diverse combination of people from around the world came together to create a true democracy. Here, multicultural and multireligious identities are woven into the fabric of this American history – out of the many, one nation forms. E pluribus unum.

The narratives of pluralism – stories of tolerance, inclusion, and participation of minorities – proliferate in accounts of American identity and range from models of assimilation and melting pots to multiculturalism and cosmopolitanism. To create the history of a United States that embraces difference, these origins stories remind us of both an *original* American promise of diversity and the *continued* progress of the nation in achieving that promise. A page from this history, a moment of storytelling that draws the lines of American pluralism, can be found in Chicago's 1893 World's Parliament of Religions held in conjunction with the World Columbian Exposition. As the name implies, the Exposition was a celebration of the quadracentennial anniversary of Columbus's discovery of the Americas. The story of discovery, it seems, is very much a part of the promise of American diversity. Its symbolic imprecision and elision reverberate through centuries of self-definition, with particularly public moments of celebration punctuating the narrative. The Parliament is one of those moments, and it functions both as *part of the story* about the pluralism of a nation (an example of progress and promise that can be referred to from the present) and as an *act of storytelling*. The Parliament, especially when understood in connection to the Columbian Exposition and its Midway Plaisance, tells the story of diversity, progress, and destiny.

Sometimes referred to as "the dawn of religious pluralism," the Parliament showcased the religions and cultures of the world on an American stage, and it is often credited with introducing eastern religions into American popular culture. Richard Hughes Seager's work on the Parliament and Exposition, *The World's Parliament of Religions: The East/West Encounter, Chicago, 1893* (1995; see also Seager 1993), sheds light on the ways that public exhibition and celebration become platforms for American storytelling. He notes that "diversity in unity" was the dominant ideal of the event's planners, who sought to highlight inclusivity, cooperation, and social progress. Speakers like Dharmapala, Soyen Shaku, and Vivekananda left the Parliament celebrities and were instrumental in the spread of eastern religions in the US in the twentieth century. This story of inclusion should not let us miss the "invisible" history of exclusion. The narrative of eastern "success" occludes the lack of African American, African, Latin American, and women's voices in the Parliament. The program designed by the Parliament's producers painted an image of Protestant triumph, discovery, and successful religious pluralism. In the Parliament's act of storytelling, the greater good of pluralism is achieved through a labor of elision – an exclusion that rendered invisible the very violence that accomplished it.

Elsewhere in 1893 Chicago, the Parliament's narrative of diversity was also on display at the Columbian Exposition. The Midway Plaisance leading to the White City was visually reinforcing this image of American identity and destiny. A grand but temporary construction made of a white plaster of Paris compound, the White City mimicked classical aesthetics while also retelling a particularly American tale of the triumph of western culture, Protestantism, and the white race. Seager explains, "Patriotic, classical and Christian signs, all infused with millennial energy, are the mythic building blocks of the White City. Its implicit meaning, conveyed in architecture, ceremony, oratory and song, was that the United States was both the new imperium, a new Greece or Rome, and a New Jerusalem, the City of God and man, toward which Christians had labored for centuries" (1995: 4). The Columbian myth of discovery and progress (and of the inevitable fall of certain, less worthy, civilizations) was on full display as visitors entered the "living museum" of the Midway Plaisance and made their way to the White City.

The journey to the White City, however, did not simply *display* race, religion, and civilization; it *constructed* these very categories as it rendered certain peoples and histories visible and invisible. Evolutionary theories fuelled the racist taxonomies that organized cultures according to a hierarchy of civilization and progress, culminating with the Anglo-American Protestant culture of the White City. People from around the world were brought to the Midway to "live" in full view of visitors. The so-called savages and primitives were at the bottom of this hierarchy (Dahomeyans, Samoans, Laps, Inuits, American Indians), followed by Near Eastern and African civilizations (Algerian, Tunisian, Turkish villages), semi-civilized, non-white, non-Christian peoples (Muslims, Hindus, Buddhists), and finally, the picturesque European ethnics (Irish, German, French, and Italian villages) (Seager 1995: 25–7). On the Midway, ethnic and racial diversity was incorporated into the Columbus myth, even as it was simultaneously excluded from the White City. E pluribus unum: out of many came one universal, white, Anglo-American, Protestant culture.

The Columbus myth, through its multitude of iterations, reveals a consistency in its very malleability. Its symbolic vagueness can be employed and referenced in a variety of ways to create and maintain visions of American identity that rely on its notions of discovery, sacrifice, progress, and destiny. These larger goals and greater goods come to the foreground to block the visibility of the violence, genocide, murder, and exploitation that paved their way. The Columbian Exposition and the Parliament make diversity visible only insofar as it fits into the timeline and taxonomy of a particular evolutionary biology. Bodies of "others" are put on display to mark a general reality of diversity and inclusion, and yet, those notions rely on the invisible presence of specific historical violence (colonial, imperial) that secured the hierarchy. The story of progress is a visible presence, the human bodies on display – however real they might have been – fade into a position farther back on the timeline, hidden from view. The past, again, is all about the present.

Both the Parliament and Columbian Exposition told a story of discovery and diversity that relied on violence and exclusion. This was the story of the *inevitable* rise of one civilization. Rather than chalk this up to an antiquated, nineteenth-century racist worldview, it is important to see that this is the story that continues to be told on the "neutral" pages of the coloring book in the American public school classroom and elsewhere. We have not abandoned these narratives. An example of this legacy can be seen in the 1988 formation of the Council for a Parliament of the World's Religions, an organization formed to "convene a centenary celebration" of the original Parliament, an event that took place in Chicago in 1993. The mission statement of the organization reads, "The Council for a Parliament of the World's Religions was created to cultivate harmony among the world's religious and spiritual communities and foster their engagement with the world and its guiding institutions in order to achieve a just, peaceful and sustainable world." If the 1893 events were themselves an attempt to move toward inclusionary politics, then the 1993 reiteration of the event re-inscribed the original with an even greater sense of accomplishment. The Council pronounced that the nation was indeed moving in the right direction – toward a Global Ethic. The twentieth-century story of the Parliament does not acknowledge failures of inclusion. It once again utilizes the strategy of rendering things visible and invisible in the service of present interests. The original Parliament becomes a moment worthy of repetition; the exclusion of the event (the racism, sexism, and religious discrimination) is made invisible in the service of a narrative of progress toward diversity.

A discussion of origins is always a discussion of authority and privilege. Writing in the 1970s, Charles Long made a similar critique of American origins stories that render minority histories invisible. His critique of American storytelling in "Civil Rights – Civil Religion: Visible People and Invisible Religion" remains insightful:

> "The mighty saga of the outward acts" is a description of the American language, a language rooted not simply in the physical conquest of space, but equally a language which is the expression of a hermeneutics of conquest and suppression. It is a cultural language that conceals the inner depths, the archaic dimensions of the dominant peoples in the country, while at the same time it renders invisible all those who fail to partake of this language and its underlying cultural experiences. The religion of the American people centers around the telling and the retelling of the mighty deeds of the white conquerors. This hermeneutic mask thus conceals the true experience of Americans from their very eyes. (1974: 214)

How is it possible to "hear" and "see" the voices and images of the invisible past – especially an invisible past that is, as Long notes, simultaneously quite present and visible, yet unacknowledged? Like Smith's coloring book page, the benign language of discovery and diversity begins to reveal itself as a much more important nation-building exercise. Origins stories of discovery and diversity both seek to sublimate the violence of their enterprise in the service of a greater good; both grant visibility only to those that fit into a particular vision of the present. Stories of discovery and diversity reveal contemporary negotiations of authority and privilege that rely on elisions of racial, national, and religious violence, even as they replicate that very violence. Smith's Columbus coloring page affirms violence as ever-present but also invisible; it serves as a warning, a threat of erasure.

In the same way, the American promise of diversity and pluralism employs an amorphous origins story to prescribe particular future behaviors. The generalized ideal of "accepting pluralism" becomes more important than the specifics of what pluralism is and how it came to be. It becomes a marker to measure progress. Thus, non-pluralist nations become targets for democratization by military means – for further violence that can be retold as sacrifice for a greater good. Our origins of discovery and diversity allow us to replicate the violence that secured them. Those who reject pluralism are labeled terrorists, just as those who reject capitalist democracy are relics of a primitive worldview. The universal vision of Columbian origins can still render invisible. The Arawak's invisibility, their absence from our coloring book pages, is a warning to those who challenge the American way of life. E pluribus unum.

Martha Smith Roberts is a PhD candidate in the Department of Religious Studies at the University of California, Santa Barbara. Her current research investigates the intersections between American religious pluralism, race, and ethnicity, and the public display of the human body in twentieth-century museums and exhibitions.

10. A Genealogy of the Past

Writing a History of Origins

Russell T. McCutcheon

As part of an event marking the contributions to the study of religion made by (the now late) Wilfred Cantwell Smith, held at the University of Toronto in the Spring of 1992, Jonathan Z. Smith presented a paper entitled "Scriptures and Histories." Soon published in a special issue of *Method & Theory in the Study of Religion* (and recently included as chapter 3 of Smith's *On Teaching Religion*), it deftly picks up on themes in the former Smith's work but expands on them considerably since, as J.Z. Smith writes near the opening of his essay: "We share last names, but not much else."

Given the impatience of the Culture on the Edge collaborative with the sorts of uncritical origins narratives that must be spun in order for scholars to make judgments about how groups change over time and place – that is, routine claims of, for instance, diaspora, which make no sense without positing a static, originary homeland, a prehistoric source from which the subsequent scattering supposedly took place, thereby providing a standard against which degrees of purity, significance, and membership can be measured – the part that seems particularly relevant in "Scriptures and Histories" is an aside not too far into the essay, based on W.C. Smith's claim that scholars of the Bible spend far too much time on studying its prehistory and not enough on its subsequent history, as the other Smith phrases it. To make the case, J.Z. Smith quickly notes that such things as theories of the compositional history of the Bible (e.g., the so-called documentary hypothesis that is used to understand the Hebrew text's origins in separate writing traditions or, say, the so-called Synoptic Problem, whereby yet other scholars try to untangle the similarities, differences, and thus compositional history of the Gospels of Matthew, Mark, and Luke) are "not tenth century B.C. or first century A.D. Palestinian artifacts, they are artifacts of the 19th and 20th century European thought." In mistaking their tools (e.g., a theory concerning the prior, but no longer existent, sources from which ancient texts arose, such as the hypothesis about the so-called

Q sayings document [i.e., Quelle, German for "source," that scholars use to satisfy *their own curiosities about things they find similar or different in the material*], from which the writers of Matthew and Luke supposedly drew large portions of their subsequent text) for natural features of the datum itself, scholars erase their own fingerprints from the object, failing to see the role that they themselves have played in making something not just interesting but also understandable.

Pressing the point further, J.Z. Smith writes:

> That is to say, the "archaic" is a discovery of the modern era. In light of this, I have often toyed with the idea of constructing a course about the west and its "others" built around the chronology of when we became interested in them. It is a significantly different timeline than the one we are accustomed to – for example, the Sumerians [would] not appear until some 70 years ago. (Smith 1992: 100)

We have here the makings of a history not of things archaic but of the fairly recent scholarly practice that has made it possible to talk about such things *as if they were* archaic: the genealogy of the discourse on origins. For now, instead of beginning the discussion of, for instance, the origins of Hinduism in the dim past of the Indus River Valley some four or five millennia ago, as pretty much every world religions textbook does in its opening pages, we'd instead begin the story in the late nineteenth century, when European scholars, colonialists, and travelers first called "it" Hindooism or even Brahmanism, during which time a series of European observations, curiosities, and eventually archeological digs (anticipated by dynamite blastings to lay track for the, yes, colonial-era East India Railway Company!) began taking place, which then made it possible to posit the existence of what we have, since then, come to know as the early Harappan Civilization which has some (or so the story goes) linear connection with that modern thing we now call Hinduism. (It would not be difficult to rethink, in precisely the same manner, the historicity of the other group important to the traditional Hinduism origins tale told by scholars: the Indo-Europeans, something Stefan Arvidsson has done rather nicely in his book, *Aryan Idols: Indo-European Mythology as Ideology and Science* [2006].) Thus, the invention of Hinduism, and tales of its origins, as a discursive object that is defined by scholars in a particular way, so as to include this or that empirically observable practice, symbol, or institution within its umbrella, is little more than a century or so old, regardless of how antique the diverse items and practices on which we draw when talking about "it" may (or may not) seem to be themselves.

On this note it is worth returning briefly to that quote by J.Z. Smith above, for it was in response to a memory he cites of a conversation with his then colleague Mircea Eliade, when Smith remarked to him how curious it was that "his beloved 'primitives' (codeword, 'archaic') had made no appearance in the first three volumes of his projected four volume *Histoire des croyances et des idées religieuses* [*A History of Religious Ideas*]." To which Eliade replied: "Because, Jonathan, they did not enter the history of the major religions until the 16th century" (Smith 1992: 99–100). It is worth stopping here for a moment to entertain the difference between two ways of talking about this topic. I have no doubt that, for those siding with Eliade here, the so-called primitives were already out there somewhere, just eluding our knowledge of them (until the so-called Age of Discovery and certain technological innovations made it possible to go find them), like the tree that we're sure fell in the forest despite no one being there to witness it. From the other point of view, the point of view that scrutinizes our production of knowledge and examines how it is that we come to know and arrange the world around us (the position I'm pressing here based on Smith's approach), there was no "they" there, within our system of knowing, until we, as observers, invented them – that is, until we defined what counted as "primitive" or "archaic" or "small scale" or "indigenous," or whatever term is fashionable at any given moment, and then used it to group certain people and practices together, in distinction from other things that we group together and call "modernity" and "civilization," there was no such distinct phenomenon, identifiable population, or bounded group. If this is the approach we adopt, one that rigorously places our own gaze, as scholars, into a particular social setting, then it is not that "they entered our history," as Eliade himself might have phrased it; instead, we start with the assumption that the impression of some distinct "they" was conjured into existence and then maintained, in specific situations, by a coordinated system of intellectual curiosity (i.e., What do "we" make of the people who were already there when we landed on the beach? Are "they" even human?), social classification (i.e., How are they like or unlike us?), ethical questions (How, then, should "we" treat "them"?), political decision-making (To what "they" are entitled? What do "we" make of "their" claims on "us"?), and even legal management (i.e., consider disputes that continue to this day over how much "native" ancestry one needs to be considered "Native American"). There are too many diverse and unfocused activities going on in that forest for us to just presume that a distinguishable thing called a tree is falling with or without us there to name it and see it, and we now see that we ourselves, driven by practical interests, play a crucial role in isolating that subject as an item to be named, examined, discussed, interacted with, and thereby isolated from innumerable related, neighboring factors, and so on. And we would be wise to work with the assumption that the people whom we make subjects of *our* study do the same to us when they come to know and arrange *their* worlds.

How, then, do we write a history of origins? Well, start with whenever you hear, or whenever you read, "In the beginning..." (or any of its variants, such as "When I was a kid...," "The Founding Fathers said...," or "The author intended..."), being sure to keep your eyes and ears on the storytellers, and the moves they make, and not get carried away by their tales. If this was our approach – a far more dynamic understanding of how discourses on the past are produced – then, as Smith suggests, we'd be writing history in significantly different ways, carrying out an archeology of the continually-changing present's discourse on the supposedly settled past.

Russell T. McCutcheon is Professor and Chair of the Department of Religious Studies at the University of Alabama. His research is about the social and political implications of competing classification systems.

Competing Christs

Brad Stoddard

In February 2014, a variety of posts clogged my Facebook and Twitter feeds for several days as many of my friends posted articles, tweeted, and otherwise commented on a recently-surfaced audio clip featuring comments made by United States Lieutenant General William G. "Jerry" Boykin. While speaking at the WallBuilders ProFamily Legislators Conference the previous Fall, Boykin made several comments about Jesus, comments that many of my friends either staunchly supported or derided as irresponsible and wrong. What exactly did he say that caused the uproar? Simply put, Boykin argued that Christians have a religious duty to arm themselves with semi-automatic weapons. He said:

> The Lord is a warrior and in Revelation 19 it says when He comes back, He's coming back as what? A warrior. A mighty warrior leading a mighty army, riding a white horse with a blood-stained white robe.... I believe that blood on that robe is the blood of His enemies 'cause He's coming back as a warrior carrying a sword. And I believe now – I've checked this out – I believe that sword He'll be carrying when He comes back is an AR-15.

According to the audio clip that documents his speech, Boykin then referenced American history to interpret the contemporary relevance of the scriptures. Jesus, Boykin argued, "was sayin' in building my kingdom you're gonna have to fight at times...and that was the beginning of the Second Amendment." For Boykin, Jesus and his warrior ethos inspired America's Founding Fathers, who crafted the Second Amendment to enshrine into the Constitution our divinely-inspired duty to build and defend Christ's kingdom with the modern version of a sword. "[T]he sword today is an AR-15," he stated, "so if you don't have one, go get one. You're supposed to have one. It's biblical."

Predictably, Boykin's comments triggered a wave of response from many of my friends across the religious and political spectrums. Several of them supported Boykin and reaffirmed his version of history. Not surprisingly, these are the same friends who have repeatedly posted status updates, articles, memes, or comments that not only oppose gun regulation, but also oppose the "liberal" government that wants to regulate guns. Embedded within their support for Boykin were a host of assumptions related to politics, the role of the government, the role of Christianity, and of course, their rights as gun owners.

Equally predictable were the responses from other friends, who collectively agreed that Boykin "got Jesus wrong." Boykin, they argued, ignored Jesus's call for compassion and to "love thy neighbor." Clearly, they asserted, you can't love your neighbor if you're armed with an AR-15 and if your robes are covered with their blood. Like Boykin, they substantiated their claims by referencing history, the Bible, and the historical Jesus; but unlike Boykin, they found a "softer" Jesus who would never ask us to arm ourselves in service of His kingdom.

After they concluded that Jesus would support gun regulation, they then addressed Boykin's comments about the Founding Fathers and the Second Amendment. Contra Boykin, they argued that America's Founding Fathers created the Second Amendment free from divine guidance or intervention. They also argued that the Second Amendment doesn't guarantee the right to own AR-15s and other semi-automatic rifles. In other words, neither Jesus, nor the Founding Fathers, nor the Second Amendment, prevent gun regulation.

My Facebook and Twitter feeds were playing out many of the issues that Russell McCutcheon has discussed in his essay, in which he calls on scholars to reconsider the ways they approach both origins narratives and the scholars (or friends on social media) who construct them. Specifically, he suggests that scholars err when they mistake contemporary tools with natural or organic features of older datum. Second, McCutcheon suggests that we should redirect our gaze away from the origins narratives and instead focus our attention on the storytellers themselves. Herein lies what I take to be McCutcheon's most important insight. For McCutcheon, history is not a fixed, stable, or otherwise "recoverable" past; rather, the storyteller's "practical interests" in the present influences his or her interpretation of the past.

With this in mind, I returned to the issue of Boykin and Jesus. Based on my friends' responses to Boykin, it appears as though the search for the "historical Jesus" and American history are inseparably tethered to our present-day interests. Without exception (at least on my Facebook and Twitter feeds), Boykin's supporters agreed that a sacred trinity of Jesus, America's Founding Fathers, and the Second Amendment supports their right to own guns, free from government regulation. In short, their interpretation of history justified their political predispositions.

The irony was lost on my more liberal friends: that they shared much more in common with Boykin than they'd like to admit. Like Boykin and his supporters, they too appealed to Jesus, America's Founding Fathers, and the Second Amendment, although their historical analyses led them to a different conclusion. Contra Boykin, their version of history justified *more* gun regulation, a position that is premised on the federal government playing a larger role in the regulation of American society.

In short, Boykin, his supporters, and his detractors all played the same game and accepted similar rules. They all appealed to history, agreed that historical narratives are relevant to the present, and interpreted that history to justify their own political positions. It thus becomes evident that the quest for history is often tethered to contemporary issues.

Brad Stoddard is an Assistant Professor of Religious Studies at McDaniel College, Westminster, Maryland. His current research examines the intersections of religion, law, and the carceral state.

Afterword

Origins Today[1]

Russell T. McCutcheon

What is origins today? I shall give at the outset a first, very simple answer: *claims of origination are a form of speech or writing and, as such, they are acts in the present for social effect in that present situation's imagined future*. Origins are therefore not about the past. The goal of the preceding essays, as well as what follows, is to try to persuade you of the utility of making this shift, from a fascination with the supposed object of the claim (i.e., the past, the ancestors, some golden age, or just the good old days, etc.), to a focus on the current speaker, the present writer, the one who is making the claim.

But how to begin, if that is my intended destination?

Perhaps I should tell a story?

Not too long ago, my wife and a good friend went to Waffle House, a popular restaurant in the American South since 1955 – an early-morning favorite of retirees and blue-collar workers looking for a good cup'a joe, as well as a late-night haunt of high school and college partygoers looking for some after-hours carbs to offset the evening's, shall we say, intake. That is, the stools at its counters, where people eat biscuits and eggs and toast and hash browns and sausages, are a piece of Americana, today populated by a curiously inter-generational mix, some of whom wear their trucker's hats ironically and intentionally and others who, being a little older, wear them, well, just because that's what they wear, I guess. And although I wasn't there for breakfast that day, I got an original, one-of-a-kind Waffle House coffee mug out of the deal.

And if you look on the bottom you see that it was made in China.

---

[1] Small portions of this Afterword draw on two separate, short blog posts from edge.ua.edu, greatly revised and elaborated. For the relevance of the title and the opening few lines, see the close to this Afterword.

So my question is: How far can one stretch the presumed originality, and thus the value, of an item before something snaps, and it all crumbles in on itself? How much can we modify a claim of uniqueness before something is judged a useless, worthless, derivative copy?

I queried my class about this a few semesters ago, back when I first got that mug, and although the room was filled with people who held the diner chain in pretty high esteem – "an American original," one might say – as embodying something specific to their experience growing up and coming of age in the US (say, stopping off at the Waffle House late one night, after a concert or maybe even their high school prom), none of them seemed bothered by the "Made in China" stamp on the bottom of the mug. Imported consumer goods, though once signifying (maybe for some of the old-timers seated on stools at the counter) poor or derivative quality in the local imagination (i.e., cheap, both in price and value), are now a fact of life in North America, and in some cases – for example, cars and electronics, neither of which are considered cheap anymore – it likely signifies for some people superior quality, despite various "Buy American" campaigns over the past few decades. (*Aside*: they're odd campaigns, if you think about it, since the global economy today means that everything is from somewhere else, whether the raw materials or the finished goods, ensuring that the so-called foreign or imported car you buy may have been assembled at a plant in the neighboring state or may be manufactured out of steel that people here exported to there in the first place – people like two of my brothers-in-law who have each had long careers in the steel industry in Canada.) But when I asked my students if Waffle House – known for its hearty breakfasts and fast service – could add noodle dishes, maybe lo mein, to their menu, well…, that's a horse of a different color, I soon learned. They expect ketchup bottles among the condiments at the tables, not low-sodium soy sauce.

So, to repeat: how far can one stretch the presumed originality, and thus the value, of an item before something snaps, and it all crumbles in on itself? How much can we modify a claim of uniqueness before something is judged a useless, worthless, derivative copy?

Is it as simple as saying (as it may very well be!) that so long as the "Made Somewhere Else" stamp is discreet and on the bottom ("out of sight, out of mind"), so long as the mug has the correct "old school diner" color and hourglass curve, and also the proper heft to it, then everything's ok? And, much as a million people feel that they can express their individuality by all dressing the same (*Aside*: you're hardly the only one wearing jeans today, but you likely still feel distinctive, no?), can a gross of identical mugs shipped to the US each look sufficiently retro, singular, original, and thus legitimate? If so, then we do indeed judge books by their covers, no? Or, instead, do we all ironically recognize that, let alone mugs, American-ness (much like self-identity being defined elsewhere, by others – by what we're not) is just as manufactured as anything else – and, lately, a lot of that manufacturing is happening in China, and we're buying it (with a lot of loans from China and elsewhere too)?

And, while I'm asking questions, just what do all those guys with the un-ironic, weathered, ball caps think of the kids at the Waffle House counter drinking coffee with their brand new trucker's caps carefully tilted at just the right jaunty angle? After all, the old guys were wearing them long before the hipsters adopted them as their own badge of status. Does being first no longer count for anything? But, come to think of it, aren't the old guys also wearing their hats in imitation of yet others, who came before them, who perhaps occupied the same class position or job as they do now, but who were there and donned those caps long before they came into Waffle House for the first time and ordered "Coffee, black"? Didn't they see, long ago, perhaps their dad, or maybe some guy in an old movie, with his shirt sleeves rolled up – but just part-way – ready to pitch in where needed, wearing a hat something like that?

If we think of it this way – that is, that it's copying, borrowing, and appropriation all the way down (making "appropriation" basically a synonym for both "history" and "culture," instead of seeing it, as many do today, as stealing; for who, after all, "owns" how to wear a hat?) – then claiming originality, being first, being authentic, is always deferrable, for no sooner than one claims to be the first then it turns out that someone was always there before you. (Christopher Columbus, after all, didn't really discover a place where lots of people were already living, right? It was new to him, his crew, and the people who financed his trip, no doubt, but hardly a New World in some deep or obvious sense.) This is why claims of being original, authentic, indigenous, etc., are all so very complicated, when we really look at them closely. Like that person talking to my father in the epigraph to this book, failing to see that his claim about the past, and how deep that snow once was, *was actually a claim about himself, as an adult, in the present*, a claim that, until my dad happened along with his witty insight, failed to take into account time and change – thus a claim that nicely normalized, or naturalized, the vantage point the person happened to occupy in the present, as if that position transcended time and space and thus shared the sort of privilege that an all-knowing narrator's voice has in a novel or a movie.

But once we realize that our knees were a lot closer to the ground when we were kids, thereby helping to explain why the snow was (*correction*: now seems to have once been) so much deeper back then, we soon realize that terms like original, indigenous, and authentic are not merely neutral descriptors of actual, long-gone states of affairs that are or are not linked to us in some peculiar way (by means of what we call tradition, lineage, heritage, inheritance, even destiny or fate). Instead, they are rhetorical tools that are used in the here and now, in discrete situations, to make something or someone stand out, to mark turf, and thus to help create the impression of status and rank in competition with others who are, more than likely, equally eager for the spotlight – as is so apparent in the now classic British comedy sketch, "The Four Yorkshiremen," that dates from the late 1960s (though probably many think of Monty Python's later version of it), in which four nostalgic upper-class gentlemen battle it out with increasingly outrageous tales of how hard they once had it as kids, all of which is pretty clearly a contest in the present, to outdo the humble beginnings of all the others, thereby securing the primacy of the rank to which they've risen today. If such tales are used the right way, in the correct setting, at the proper moment, and in support of interests that your readers or listeners share, then maybe no one will go digging to see who was there before your ship came ashore or to find out who had it even worse than you. But if done in the wrong way – "Right. I had to get up in the morning at ten o'clock at night half an hour before I went to bed, drink a cup of sulphuric acid, work twenty-nine hours a day down mill, and pay mill owner for permission to come to work, and when we got home, our Dad and our mother would kill us and dance about on our graves singing 'Hallelujah'." – then it authorizes nothing and we just laugh.

Speaking of digging, it just occurred to me that those potatoes they're frying up at Waffle House, for the dish we commonly call hash browns, well, we all know – don't we? – that the English name for those stem tubers is originally of Spanish derivation (*patata*), itself derived, scholars think, from yet other Caribbean and South American linguistic precursors, and that the things themselves are commonly traced to South America, long prior to exploration, colonialism, and trade eventually sending them worldwide in ever-increasing variety. So why, I'd like to ask, are they not shelved in the "Ethnic Food" aisle that's now so often found in our local grocery stores, along with, for instance, the Curry Ketchup from Germany (though curry, of course, names a host of spices associated first with South Asia; and as for that slice of Americana called ketchup? Well, they think it first came from China…). It appears that the issue, then, is not just how far can one stretch the presumed authenticity, the originality, and the singularity, of an item before something snaps but, conversely, how long does it take us to become so accustomed to the exotic, the alien, the strange, and the new that we begin to see it as local, familiar, and thus old and inconsequential? When do we roll up our sleeves and dig for the distant origins – as a late nineteenth-century anthropologist might have once done, saying, "We can explain those modern-day survivals that we know as superstition; for instance, originally, people threw salt over their shoulder because..." – and when do we just sit at the diner's counter and put ketchup on our fries?

But in order to draw my readers' attention to what origins discourses are up to, I have just implicated myself (as I did in the opening to this very volume, where I described the origins of the Culture on the Edge initiative) in all this by spinning my own tale of origins – did you catch it?

"[T]he English name for those stem tubers is originally of Spanish derivation...."

Though maybe catching me playing along is just as it should be – whether we like it or not, we're all stuck in language, in society, in contests with many others (all with varying interests and goals) over place and identity, all of us thereby inhabiting ambiguous situations in which we are judged alike but also unlike so many other things around us. ("[I]s there a mythology of the mythologist? No doubt" – wrote the French semiotician, Roland Barthes.) But how to sort this all out? Well, perhaps we should consider re-describing identity claims – for example, "I am human" or "We are happy" or "They came from there" – as the sum result of all those deftly arranged and managed relations of similarity and difference. Managing these ambiguous situations, drawing attention to just some similarities and ignoring all others, focusing on certain differences and forgetting all others, establishing links between otherwise disparate items (such as those things we call "causes" or "influences"), creating both coalitions and schisms, thus seems to be the day-to-day business of identification – a business of which claims to origins and originality are but a part.

I think here of a point made by the French scholar who was the founder of school of thought that first took hold in anthropology in the mid-twentieth century, and then in a wide variety of other academic fields, known as Structuralism. As described by Jonathan Z. Smith:

> Claude Lévi-Strauss has recalled, on a number of occasions, a Proust-like reverie triggered by contemplating a dandelion one Sunday in May, 1940.... In order to "see" the dandelion, Lévi-Strauss discovered, one must, at the same time, "see" the other plants which

differ from it. The dandelion cannot be "intelligible" by itself, but only as "much more," as constituted by the totality of those relations of similarities and differences that allow one to "isolate" it.... [D]enomination is placed in relation to classification, as it must be.... Lévi-Strauss [thus]...insists that classification, comparison and naming be seen as a single, indissoluble process.... [O]bjects are "given" as "bundles of relations" as part of the process of intellection itself. (Smith 2000: 35)

This bundling of relations, this structure of managed similarity and difference that we eventually come to see *as* "the dandelion" (or insert your preferred identity here), which is itself the product of judgments, tastes, preferences, interests, etc., driving this process of focusing, organizing, and overlooking, also results in everything from failing to "see" just how exotic potatoes can be to adamantly claiming to be the first to wear a certain hat in a certain way – it is business as usual when it comes to standing out from the crowd in this or that way, to staking a claim to occupying a certain sort of place, to tracing one's lineage from a specific source (and not any of the many others from which you no doubt could also have imagined yourself descending), and to occupying a specific place for a specific period of time. The question, then, is whether, as scholars, we – like Lévi-Strauss or maybe even like my father talking about the snowy past – can see this happening, at least some of the time, and, if so, whether we are able to make the choices, the conditions, and the consequences of this identification process – that is, the bundling of relations – apparent instead of just taking it for granted, as if it just happens to us?

To begin to do this – and by "this" I mean work with this volume's authors to recover the current choices and situations by further complicating how we understand what's being done by that specific identification technique that goes by the name of origins tales (whether they are about the universe or your family) – we first need to make a shift towards seeing our own fingerprints on our object of study, thereby combating the tendency to think that we work with immaculate, obviously interesting things that just came into the world, somewhat magically, of their own accord. It's a necessary shift if we're to start seeing the origins narratives that we tell and retell today – "Why, when I was a kid..." – as doing something other than neutrally describing, from an objective, independent, or disinterested distance, settled past processes of obvious and deeply abiding significance, that – much like a cherished baton in a relay race – are propelled forward from some distant past to the unsuspecting present.

To make this shift, consider a pop song from 1998; contrary to those who might look down on studying items from so-called popular culture (like those diner mugs, perhaps) in favor of studying things that are somehow thought to be authoritatively old, intellectually compelling, and thus naturally significant (yes, I'm talking to you if you thought this essay would naturally be all about myths of origins and cross-cultural creation tales [i.e., cosmogonies, as the specialists call them – see McCutcheon 2000 if that's your interest]), pop songs are as relevant as any other item of cultural/identity production and strike me as sometimes containing memorable nuggets of social theory. So a few lyrics have stuck with me over the years, such as a line about the temptation towards (and dangers of) nostalgia from Don Henley's "The Boys of Summer" (1984), when he sings about being on the road and seeing a Dead-head bumper sticker on the back of a Cadillac. (A "Dead-head," of course, is the self-adopted name for fans of the once prominent, non-mainstream rock band, The Grateful Dead – a band much associated with non-commercial values, making the appearance of that sticker on a luxury car something worth noticing, perhaps.) As I went on to write elsewhere about this example,

> ...the singer reflects on how he thought to himself that one can never look back, suggesting not only that he ought not turn around to look at the car but that, as made evident in the famous title of Thomas Wolfe's 1940 novel, you can't go back home again. Therefore, it is rather ironic that a luxury car bears a totem best associated with a critique of the kind of status and excessive consumption that the car (and its owner's lifestyle, I presume) represents. However, despite his admonition, [the nostalgia of] "looking back"...is the fuel of social formation. By symbolically re-embodying a moment when the group recalls itself to have been politically marginal, under attack, alienated in practical, material terms, and thus forced to engage in extreme forms of physical behavior either as a form of political protest, social experimentation, or actual combat, a small number of contemporary group members and ritual specialists can portray a onetime social trauma for their now satiated and well healed peers – a time when "they" too [or at least those who they now claim as their predecessors] were hungry and marginalized. It is a technique that seemingly allows one to leap outside oneself,...backward into a very specific past so as to symbolically destabilize, and thus re-energize, the now normalized present, thus...propelling forward a renewed sense of the group and the self within the group. "*We* were once in Egypt..." [as told in the Jewish Passover narrative]. Neither the Other nor this past is some authoritative archetype.... Like the bumper sticker on the Cadillac, it

is a discursive device in the present that juxtaposes [present] security with [once past and, you never know, possibly returning] insecurity, as a means for destabilizing the apparent sense of having arrived by holding out one's eventual destination as if it was perpetually beyond one's reach. (McCutcheon 2003: 120–1)

But the song that I have in mind now is Semisonic's 1998 hit "Closing Time." It's a simple song about the last dance and the last call at a bar, and what opportunities might present themselves for later…, if you're lucky, I guess. While its "you don't have to go home but you can't stay here" line may have stuck in some people's minds, for me it was another, at the end of the song:

> Every new beginning
> comes from some other
> beginning's end.

This, to me, is a pretty significant statement of what we might call an anti-origins discourse – the awareness that what we imply by the term "history" is not a simple narrative of obviously existing past deeds or events that had their start somewhere back there and follow a pre-set cause/ effect order to us today but, instead, an awareness that we should bring to our studies the presumption that the things we take for granted as settled, as established, *could have been otherwise* – because, simply (or crassly?) put, "shit happens" and the bundle, the identity, the outcome that results, could have been rather different. It is to be aware that some unforeseen circumstance – a fire in the Town Hall perhaps? – could have easily eliminated all of the records and thus all of the material evidence of a birth, a marriage, a transaction, a death. And thus the past that we thought we knew, upon which we based our sense of who we are today, has suddenly been irreparably altered; there are no backups to those documents (and even if there are, do you trust the transcription? Were errors introduced in the re-production process? Is the handwritten legible – "Is that a 1 or a 7 on the birth certificate"?); in other words, once destroyed, it becomes idle speculation whether something prior to us really did happen or not – ask the disoriented people combing through the debris of their home, after a flood, after a hurricane, unsure of *who* they now are, *where* they now are, even *why* they now are, given the sudden absence of the many totems that once surrounded them on their walls, their bookcases, their end tables – thereby revising the past by changing the present. In this way, yesterday can now be understood as a continual reinvention of today, making the past an ongoing work-in-progress, for what gets to count as a starting point, as the origins of this or that, is always a judgment made in the present, on the part of the storyteller, the one who anchors a tale by starting out, "Well, I was born in a small town..." – a tale that now has all the makings of either a triumphal narrative of accomplishment over adversity or a nostalgic yarn for purer, simpler times. However, we won't know which until we know more about the situation of the one telling the tale, and the effect he or she may hope these words to have on the listeners.

If this is the shift that we make, then apart from now seeing ourselves in line with a writer such as Emile Durkheim, among the first proponents of sociology, who – distancing his early twentieth-century sociology from those who came just before, for example those late nineteenth-century anthropologists whom we today call Intellectualists, who tried to account for contemporary social processes and practices in terms of their non-testable speculations on archaic origins, distance meaning, or remote purpose – famously wrote in 1912 that "if by origin [of religion] one means an absolute beginning, there is nothing scientific about the question, and it must be resolutely set aside" (1995: 7), we have also arrived at, thanks to that lyric from "Closing Time," the helpful distinction between origins and beginnings, at least as made by the late literary critic, Edward Said. For as Said writes:

> beginning is basically an activity which ultimately implies return and repetition rather than simple linear accomplishment, that beginning and beginning-again are historical whereas origins are divine....
> (1985: xvii)

As he uses these two key terms, beginnings and origins – a use reminiscent of the Nietzsche-informed, Foucault-fuelled distinction between merely writing a *history* (a sequential narrative leading from the past-as-cause to the present-as-effect) and a *genealogy* (an effort to name the conditions that make talking about such things as the past, the self, justice, sanity, etc., possible in the first place) – claims about beginnings are active, presuming some process whereby prior events result in subsequent happenings; whereas claims of origins, or of origination, are passive, that is, something supposedly just comes into existence (Poof!), somewhat akin to the passive voice which seems to ascribe no intentionality or agency to the actions it describes (e.g., saying "He was killed..." as opposed to "So-and-so killed him...") or how scholars a few centuries ago thought things like flies came into being (a theory – if that's even the right word for it – once known as spontaneous generation). Or what about Intelligent Design advocates today, who claim that some things in the world are just too complex to have resulted from prior components (i.e., their disagreement with a theory of origins called evolution) and thus had to have *just appeared on the scene, fully formed*, thanks to some Intelligent Designer whom they might as well just call God. Instead, the active voice, as well as the way we commonly use the word "beginning" – as in "A was the beginning of B" – puts the emphasis not on the result (accompanied, perhaps, by a triumphant "Ta-Daaaa!") but, instead, on the various preconditions and the mechanisms of change and transmission themselves.

So we have here a choice, between a discourse on origination (despite the common English translation, "In the beginning," of what is probably one of the best known origins tales for some readers, the opening words to the Book of Genesis) and a discourse on beginnings (i.e., like the Waffle House mug, everything is from somewhere else). Whereas the latter is a narrative of how something is dependent on something else, the former is a discourse on singularity and uniqueness, hence the link between talk of origins and claiming something or someone to "be an original" – to be one of a kind, unencumbered by precedents.

If we side with Durkheim – leaving others to speculate on distant and themselves uncaused big bangs of all sorts – and start from the assumption that it is contingency all the way down (happenstance, things could have been different, every ending is a new beginning of some sort, etc.), assuming that there was always a complex variety of things here already, from which the present resulted, then it makes sense that the alternative approach, an origins narrative, itself becomes very curious to us inasmuch as it claims to isolate *this* specifically and not *that* from out of the busy, ambiguous past, as if the object, the point in time, that attracts our attention is somehow a pristine, uncaused moment that stands out on its own…, a claim that bears no trace of any of our fingerprints, our choices, our priorities in selecting just that moment. (*Question*: do things *attract* our attention, as if they have a magnetism or gravitation – in a word, agency – all their own, or would it be more accurate to say that *our* interests make them objects of attention, thereby putting us in the driver's seat and not the objects? After all, as Louis Althusser once understood so well [naming the process "interpellation"], one *becomes* a suspect only once one is suspected by someone else, no?) To rephrase, an origins narrative is effective because, in keeping the listener's eye on the object of the story (e.g., bygone snowfalls) and not the subject telling the tale (e.g., the person talking to my father about his childhood memories), it erases these choices, overlooks the effort to create a certain set of relationships, thereby eliminating all evidence that "it could have been otherwise" and, instead, *portraying some result as not being a result at all*, but, rather, as necessary, as inevitable, as pre-existent, as static, as natural, and thus as always and already significant, regardless of our role in the whole exercise.

However, a beginnings narrative, what I'm calling an anti-origins discourse, is far more useful to us as scholars if we are intent on studying people and the things they do, because (1) it presumes that the past is filled with innumerable, ambiguous prior things, so much so that we'd call it *over-signified* or *over-determined*, for its elements mean (or can come to mean) far too much and far too many different, even contradictory, things; and therefore (2) it is an approach that puts us in the position of recognizing that we, as agents in the present who have interests, who are members of groups that taught us things without our asking (thus making us both agents with volition and intention *but also* products of prior structures and collaborations not of our making), *must choose*, in the continually changing here-and-now, what to pay attention to, which generic item will count as junk and which will count as an antique, what will be judged as an insignificant or forgettable habit and what shall become a noteworthy tradition that must be rehearsed and conserved because we today think it conveys meaning and significance. Beginnings narratives, then, keep the tellers of the tale in focus, making us curious about their choices and agendas, the things of their world that they take for granted and seek to conserve by looking over the available evidence in that archive we call the past and deciding to start their tale here and not there, creating mutually beneficial patterns and precedents, by connecting just these and not those events into the developmental narrative they tell, a story that has a pre-selected beginning, a middle, and a culminating end.

For instance, when I'm trying to illustrate this very point I sometimes ask my students "How was your day?" and then wait for them quickly – so quickly that I'm sure they are unaware of it until I later draw it to their attention, making them their own object of study – to sift through what of their day they now happen to recall (*Question*: who remembers what they did at 9:03:56 that morning? Or at 9:04:38?), select some narrative elements, string them together, and then simplistically assess them as either good or bad, so as to casually reply, "I've had a good day." But instead of taking that reply as our starting point, as a pristine, naturally occurring item in our environment, or even as if it is either an accurate or inaccurate description of the day, the trick is to build back up to it from scrutinizing selections and judgments, targeting students in the present moment, caught in the situation of having to answer my query, and seeing them as the arbiters of what in their no doubt complex, largely forgotten, past *will get to count as memorable* (good or bad), seeing them as the ones who then arrange and bundle the elements, and as the ones who eventually come to a conclusion concerning their value *to them now* – choices and decisions all inevitably taking place under the pressure of the unpredictable present (where people like me ask them unanticipated questions like this). For it is a present prone to change – as the coyote in the old Road Runner cartoons knows only too well, when things suddenly spin out of control and, to his chagrin, he finds himself hanging, for a brief moment, past the cliff's edge, while his rocket-powered roller skates run out of steam, just before he plummets straight down to a small doughnut-shaped puff of dust when he lands.

Thus the indeterminate present continually reinvents the past in the service of authorizing that very present as if it was determinate, necessary, everlasting.

There may be no better example of this – to stick with our focus on the theoretical utility of taking pop culture seriously – than a March 29, 2005 episode (season 1, episode 2, entitled "Diversity Day") of the US adaptation of the (originally!) British television series *The Office* that, like that earlier lyric, has stuck with me, perhaps because of the sophisticated theoretical point it makes (or maybe it's just about the sentimentalism that it inspires?). Jim Halpert, the likable paper salesman who is secretly in love with Pam Beesly, the receptionist (and she with him as well), has a terrible day in which he is repeatedly interrupted while trying to make an annual sales call that always results in a quarter of his year's commission. When he finally gets through to the client, after repeated delays and frustrations from his workmates, it turns out that his arch nemesis in the office, Dwight Schrute, has already made the call, has made the sale – and has made the commission. It's a horrible day for poor Jim, something more than apparent to him and to the viewer.

But…, at the end of the work day, after participating in what turns out to be an inane training session at work, Pam, who happens to have been seated next to Jim in the conference room, falls asleep with her head gently resting on his shoulder.

> The meeting ends.
>
> The room empties.
>
> Alone, they remain.
>
> He looks at the camera, unsure what to do.
>
> He softly wakes her.

She rises, a little chagrined, fixing her hair.

She leaves.

He remains, alone.

From there we cut to the confessional-shot, where the actor, seated alone in a spare office, sometimes speaks directly to the filmmakers, in character, debriefing on the day's events. And now we learn that what had been a terrible day has suddenly been utterly transformed, in a way he could have never imagined hours or even just moments before:

"Umm..., not a bad day..."
he says with a small but self-satisfied grin.

Abracadabra, the past has changed, right before our eyes, inasmuch as the focus and the priorities of the speaker, the chooser, the one actively (and not passively) making and unmaking the connections in that bundle of relations of similarity and difference, has himself changed.

So the seemingly inconsequential question "How was your day?" – not unlike a simple pop lyric or a mug from Waffle House – becomes an opportunity to examine rather complex procedures in the *contingent present* (one that is always changing, one that – as both Jim and the coyote know only too well – could easily have been otherwise) that create the impression of an authorized, inevitable moment (i.e., what we might call representations of the present as-it-necessarily-must-be), inasmuch as the selection of just this originary reference point, coupled with connecting just these elements to comprise a particular sort of developmental narrative that gets us from there/then to here/now, is completely obscured, much as Jim, in the light of the unexpectedly tender moment, suddenly forgets his missed sale and lost income. The fingerprints are thereby rubbed clean and there's no trace of the choosers and the organizers. It just happened that way, we tell ourselves. There's nothing I could have done about it. It's natural. So don't blame me. I'm not responsible. It was destiny. Kismet. We knew all along. That's just the way it is.

But an anti-origins discourse, one that probes the present for possible reasons why each past is collected and portrayed as it is, leading to different sorts of todays, and newly possible tomorrows, comprises what I would call a historical consciousness. And this is what I hear in that lyric, and this is what I see in the television show's invitation for us to peer into Jim's life – not a Romantic nostalgia for the past or some mystical sense of samsara going 'round and 'round, but, instead, the more basic posture, adopted by the preceding essays, that focuses on the happenstance along with the interested factors that made it possible to talk or act or think about, or organize, the thing that we call the past or an origin.

My good friend Willi Braun, a scholar of Christian origins who has thought carefully about that word "origins" in his disciplinary identity, tells a story about storytelling, one that nicely illustrates the point we've now arrived at in my thoughts on the place of origins today:

> A while ago, my daughter was assigned by her literature teacher to write a snippet from her past: a limited exercise in autobiography. She asked me to read it, and, though I recognized the event described in her narrative, it struck me as highly invented. Moods, motives, detailed thought processes of the past were neatly dramatized and, by means of literary fictioning, tethered to a single theme. "Is this how it really was?" I asked. "No," she conceded, "I couldn't remember how it actually was, and the teacher told me that the story must have a theme, and so I made some things up so I could write a story." "But," she continued, "the story is true, it really is about me." (Just as, incidentally, the anecdote I have just told is a product of fictioning the facts of the conversation with my daughter!) *Factere* [Latin: to do, to make] and *fingere* [Latin: to fashion or form, as also applied to the truth] may be "distant cousins" but in my daughter's activity on the past they seemed to have romanced each other, indeed married each other to become a single process of narrative re-presentation, such that the result was a fictioned factual story, a "believed-in imagining" (Sarbin 1998) about the past. Anyone who has tried to write her or his autobiography, or has served as a church or town historian will probably recognize at least some truth in what I am talking about. Artificiality thus is not something to be avoided in historical production; on the contrary, history is the result of an artificializing human activity. (Braun 1999: 5)

Recovering (or better put, owning up to) our sense of this crafting of the past – both in the sense of making something but also in the sense of being strategic and wily in the making (i.e., being crafty in both senses of the word) – is what it means to historicize something, at least as I use the term. ("Always historicize!" wrote the literary critic Fredric Jameson in the opening words to his well-known book, *The Political Unconscious* [1981].) For we, as scholars in the human sciences, start with the presumption that everything comes from something, though that something might not always be apparent to us, and we are therefore suspicious of pristine originations and big bangs. But when we can find the choices, when we are able to identify alternatives that might have been, or ways in which the selection of starting points serves present needs, then we will find, I think, that – to quote Braun again – "[o]bserving the processes at work in this sort of elongated chronology of production puts us in a good position to think deeply about the question why we invest so much in the past and why it is so important that the past looks just so, rather than just any old way, and why it is apparently necessary to forget as much as we remember [when we talk about the past], and why what and how we remember is not so much a matter of 'the past' as it is a matter of *our* present."

And picking up on the significance of that plural possessive pronoun, "our," Braun elaborates, to conclude his essay (and I quote at length):

> This "our" is most important. If history [both the doing and the writing, i.e., fashioning of it]…is a human production from beginning to end, then there is no place to hide from the imperative to take responsibility for history, both in terms of our lived doings in the present and in terms of how we describe and use "the past" to rationalize our doings, worldviews, social arrangements, and the multitudinous instrumentalities, material and symbolic, by which we contrive powerful tangible worlds in accordance with our imagined worlds. There are no proxies – slippery abstractions such as "nature," "teleology," "God," "Devil," that are reified, i.e., endowed by human imagination with a rock-solid concreteness, and placed in tamper-proof, beyond-argument creeds and canons – which might allow us to avoid exercising our franchise, to cast our vote, as frankly and transparently as we can. Please, do not misunderstand: I am not implicitly pleading for a Promethean view of human performance, which by heroic dint and huff, can unfix and refix the theater of our lives at will. That would be to fall under another spell of fantasy, one which overlooks the complexities of the cultural and material forms and forces that place constraints both on the potential (power) and forms of human doing. No, the point of this little discourse…is precisely to begin to expose the complexities of history…. (1999: 6)

Indeed; the point of this little discourse, this little book, is precisely to begin to expose the complexities of talking about origins.

So, in keeping with the spirit of Braun's call for taking responsibility not only for the doings but also for how we fashion our narratives *of* those doings (which is but another one of the doings, of course: selecting, ignoring, associating, in a word, what I've been calling bundling) – where they came from and where they are going – let me end this concluding essay in a volume on origins with a quotation from at least what I now consider, in hindsight, to have been one of the first things that got me thinking this way about how it is that we make meaning, make identity, create a sense of place. It is a book that I recall discovering – well…, at least it was new *to me* – by reading yet another book that cited it, that tethered its own argument (as I've done myself!) by deferring to it: Roland Barthes's collection of little essays that originally appeared as newspaper pieces (the blog of his day?), each on a curious aspect of modern culture, entitled *Mythologies*. In the Preface we read:

> The starting point of these reflections was usually a feeling of impatience at the sight of the "naturalness" with which newspapers, art and common sense constantly dress up a reality which, even though it is the one we live in, is undoubtedly determined by history. In short, in the account given of our contemporary circumstances, I resented seeing Nature and History confused at every turn, and I wanted to track down, in the decorative display of what-goes-without-saying, the ideological abuse which, in my view, is hidden there. (Barthes 1972: 11)

However, deferring to Barthes's starting point (his Preface, his "speaking before") not only marks where this Afterword ends (though, as signaled in my opening footnote, my beginning – my very title and even my opening sentence – already deferred plainly to the ending of his little but immensely influential book), but also marks where others can begin to use this approach for themselves, to make sense of items in the world that are animated by their curiosity, as has been done by the chapters in this volume. My hope is that the shift modeled across this book – seeing claims of origins always as a style of discourse in the present, a way of doing something with words that has consequences for how we imagine the present as well as the future, whether our concern is with the gods or national political figures or coffee beans and children's coloring books – signals that, as scholars, there's a different sort of dance we could all be doing the next time we hear someone tell a story about how deep the snow used to be. For claims about the past are not necessarily about the past – as we learned earlier in this volume, it never really was about the pink shirt.

Russell T. McCutcheon is Professor and Chair of the Department of Religious Studies at the University of Alabama. His research is about the social and political implications of competing classification systems.

References

Althusser, L. (2001 [1971]). "Ideology and Ideological State Apparatuses (Notes towards an Investigation," in *Lenin and Philosophy and Other Essays*, 86–126. New York: Monthly Review Press.

Appadurai, A. (2006) "Disjuncture and Difference in the Global Culture Economy," in Meenakshi Gigi Durham and Douglas M. Kellner, eds., *Media and Cultural Studies: KeyWorks* (rev. ed.), 584–603. Malden, MA: Blackwell.

Arvidsson, S. (2006). *Aryan Idols: Indo-European Mythology as Ideology and Science*. Chicago: University of Chicago Press.

Baldwin, J. (1966). "Unnameable Objects, Unspeakable Crimes," in *The White Problem in America*, pp. 174–5. Chicago: Johnson.

Barthes, R. (1972 [1957). *Mythologies*. Selected and trans. Annette Lavers. New York: Hill and Wang, a division of Farrar, Straus, and Giroux.

Bayart, J.-F. (2005 [1996]). *The Illusion of Cultural Identity*. Trans. Steven Randall, Janet Roitman, Cynthia Schoch, and Jonathan Derrick. Chicago, IL: The University of Chicago Press.

Blight, D.W. (2001). *Race and Reunion: The Civil War in American Memory*. Cambridge, MA: Harvard University Press.

Braun, W. (1999). "Amnesia in the Production of (Christian) History," *Bulletin of the Council of Societies for the Study of Religion* 28(1), 3–8.

Collins, Suzanne (2008). *The Hunger Games*. New York: Scholastic Press.

Durkheim, E. (1995 [1912]). *The Elementary Forms of Religious Life*. Trans. and intro. Karen Field. New York: The Free Press.

Guare, J. (1994). *Six Degrees of Separation* (2nd ed.). New York: Vintage Books.

Jameson, F. (1981). *The Political Unconscious: Narrative as a Socially Symbolic Act*. Ithaca, NY: Cornell University Press.

Lilback, P.A. (2006). *George Washington's Sacred Fire: King of Prussia*. Philadelphia, PA: Providence Forum Press.

Lincoln, B. (1996). "Theses on Method," *Method & Theory in the Study of Religion* 8(3), 225–7. http://dx.doi.org/10.1163/157006896X00323.

Long, C. (1974). "Civil Rights – Civil Religion: Visible People and Invisible Religion," in R. Richey, ed., *American Civil Religion*, 211–22. New York: Harper & Row.

McCutcheon, R. (2000). "Myth," in Willi Braun and Russell T. McCutcheon, eds., *Guide to the Study of Religion*, 190–208. London: Continuum.

McCutcheon, R. (2003). *The Discipline of Religion: Structure, Meaning, Rhetoric*. New York and London: Routledge. http://dx.doi.org/10.4324/9780203451793.

Miller, Arthur (1949). *Death of a Salesman*. New York: Viking Press.

Neville, R.C., ed. (2000). *Religious Truth: A Volume in the Comparative Religious Ideas Project*. Albany, NY: State University of New York Press.

Nietzsche, Friedrich (2001 [1882]). *The Gay Science*. Ed. Bernard Williams. Cambridge, UK: Cambridge University Press.

Said, E. (1985 [1975]). *Beginnings: Intention and Method*. New York: Basic Books.

Sarbin, T.R. (1998). "Believed-in Imaginings: A Narrative Approach," in Joseph de Rivera and Theodore R. Sarbin, eds., *Believed-in Imaginings: The Narrative Construction of Reality*, 15–30. Washington, DC: American Psychological Association.

Seager, R. (1993). *The Dawn of Religious Pluralism: Voices from the World's Parliament of Religions, 1893*. Peru, IL: Open Court.

Seager, R. (1995). *The World's Parliament of Religions: The East/West Encounter, Chicago, 1893*. Bloomington, IN: Indiana University Press.

Senior, J. (2013). "In Conversation: Antonin Scalia," *The New Yorker* (October 6). http://nymag.com/news/features/antonin-scalia-2013-10/ (accessed February 20, 2014).

Smith, Jonathan Z. (1982). *Imagining Religion: From Babylon to Jonestown*. Chicago: The University of Chicago Press.

Smith, J.Z. (1992). "Scriptures and Histories," *Method & Theory in the Study of Religion* 4(1), 97–105. http://dx.doi.org/10.1163/157006892X00084.

Smith, J.Z. (2000). "Classification," in Willi Braun and Russell T. McCutcheon, eds., *Guide to the Study of Religion*, 35–44. London: Continuum.

Smith, J.Z. (2012). *On Teaching Religion*. Ed. Christopher Lehrich. New York: Oxford University Press.

Talbot, M. (2005). "Supreme Confidence: The Jurisprudence of Justice Antonin Scalia," *The New Yorker* (March 28), 40–55.

Trouillot, M.-R. (1995). *Silencing the Past: Power and the Production of History*. Boston, MA: Beacon Press.

Zinn, H. (2003 [1980]). *A People's History of the United States. 1492–Present*. New York: HarperCollins.

Suggested Films

Adaptation. DVD. Directed by Spike Jonze. Sony Pictures, 2002.
> *Adaptation* centers around a screenwriter's inability to faithfully adapt the original text of a book about orchids. The film abounds with speculations on origins, authenticity, identity, and evolution.

Avalon. DVD. Directed by Barry Levinson. TriStar Pictures, 1990.
> The engaging story of an extended family's immigration from Europe to the US city of Baltimore in the early twentieth century, and how their social relationships change over time, in step with the changing social, political, and economic

conditions of their world. The movie opens and echoes throughout with a tale of origins – "I came to America in 1914…," as told and routinely repeated by one of the family's patriarchs, suggesting the link between origins and identity.

Eternal Sunshine of the Spotless Mind. DVD. Directed by Michel Gondry. Focus Features, 2004.

This film illustrates, via a love story turned sour, the intimate relationship between identity and memory and how the significance of the past is often constructed in the present.

eXistenZ. DVD. Directed by David Cronenberg. Dimension Films, 1999.

Set a short time in our future, the story involves a radical realist movement seeking to assassinate virtual game designers, at a time when gaming is so sophisticated that it blurs the line between fiction and reality. Much more sophisticated than *The Matrix*, *eXistenZ* presses the issue as to whether reality is itself the game that we're all already playing.

F is for Fake. DVD. Directed by Orson Welles. Specialty Films, 1973.

Part documentary, part beguiling tale, it tells the story of a world-renowned art forger and his biographer (who is himself later found to be a literary forger). It is told by the actor/director – Welles himself – who at the start says: "For the next hour, everything you hear from us is really true and based on solid fact." Ironically, the film, which explores what it means to be true, original, and authentic, is more than an hour long.

The Great Silence (Il Grande Silenzio). DVD. Directed by Sergio Corbucci, 1968.

A mute gunslinger is hired to avenge the death of a woman's husband, and must come up against ruthless bounty hunters. In stark contrast to many Italian films of the genre that were made around this time (so-called Spaghetti Westerns), Corbucci's film represents the bounty hunters not as admirable, but as agents of cruelty and evil. In this way, Corbucci criticizes the Westerns for their romanti-cization of bounty hunters and mischaracterization of past events through such simplistic and one-dimensional renderings.

Jerry Maguire. DVD. Directed by Cameron Crowe. Sony Pictures Home Entertainment, 1996.

A disillusioned sports agent develops a nostalgia for simpler, more authentic approach to his work, and reignites his passion for his profession, losing it all in the process but, one could say, regaining even more in the end.

Memento. DVD. Directed by Christopher Nolan. Summit Entertainment, 2000.

A man with anterograde amnesia seeks the person who murdered his wife, but has difficulty doing so because he is unable to store new memories. By inscribing things he wants to remember on post-it notes and on his own body every day, he begins to fabricate a version of the past in order to avenge his wife's death.

Midnight in Paris. DVD. Directed by Woody Allen. Sony Pictures Home Entertainment, 2011.

The protagonist, a writer in our present, is nostalgic about 1920s Paris when a variety of now famous writers, many of whom were American, found inspiration

in the City of Lights. Wandering the streets of the city every night, he is myste-
riously transported back in time, to meet these writers and refine his own work
through their comments on it, until he realizes that nostalgia for a golden age,
for a previous moment that lends meaning to the now – in a word, a nostalgia
for an origin – is not about the past at all but about the present.

Rashomon. DVD. Directed by Akira Kurosawa. Daiei Film Co., 1950.
This classic of Japanese cinema concerns a crime that took place on the road
in eleventh-century Japan. Each participant or observer has a rather different
tale, all of which are recounted by someone who witnessed their testimonies.
The movie poses, but does not resolve, problems associated with notions of
authorship, intention, and the self-involved nature of tales concerning the past.

Suggested Readings

Almond, P.C. (1988). *The British Discovery of Buddhism*. Cambridge: Cambridge
University Press. http://dx.doi.org/10.1017/CBO9780511598210.
This is a book about origins, but not in the traditional sense. Philip Almond
describes how the concerns of Victorian-era British influenced their interpretation of "Buddhist history." *The British Discovery of Buddhism* is therefore a
case study on how various circumstances influence the way in which an object
or idea is interpreted.

Althusser, L. (2001 [1971]). "Ideology and Ideological State Apparatuses (Notes
towards an Investigation)," in *Lenin and Philosophy and Other Essays*, 86–126.
New York: Monthly Review Press.
A classic essay that not only complicates earlier Marxist notions of base and
superstructure but also introduces the notion of interpellation: the process by
which an identity, instead of being an original and permanent acquisition of the
person, is ascribed by another in discrete situations and thereby constituted in
the very act of his/her being named as a particular sort of person – for example,
the identity of "suspect" being constituted and internalized in the very moment
that a police officer calls out the person's name.

Anderson, B. (1983). *Imagined Communities: Reflections on the Origin and Spread
of Nationalism*. London: Verso.
In a work widely considered among the top current studies of nationalism,
Anderson defines the modern nation-state as a type of "imagined community,"
or socially constructed national identity formulated by those who understand
themselves to be part of its design and function. The imagined national
community is understood not only as generally cohesive, but also as intimately
tied to specific political and economic ends. While one may question the
practical plausibility of such cohesion, Anderson's influential contribution
retains a position of integral importance within conversations regarding the
origins of modern nationalism and constructions of national identity.

Barthes, R. (1972 [1957]). *Mythologies.* Selected and trans. Annette Lavers. New York: Hill and Wang, a division of Farrar, Straus, and Giroux.

In this essential study of popular culture, Barthes illustrates how a process he terms myth re-presents historically contingent phenomena as naturally occurring truths, obscuring the political and contested character of knowledge. The book is among a small number of early classics in the science that we today call semiotics (the study of signification and sign systems).

Baudrillard, J. (1995 [1991]). *The Gulf War Did Not Take Place.* Bloomington, IN: Indiana University Press.

A controversial little book, for some, that argues that the Gulf War (1990–1), as it was perceived in the popular imagination (in which Iraq invaded Kuwait), was itself an item of discourse different from the violence that was taking place, making "the Gulf War" a media and rhetorical event that selected, ignored, and narrativized raw events, in order to signify them in a manner that suited the purposes of those telling the tales.

Brundage, W. Fitzhugh (2008). *The Southern Past: A Clash of Race and Memory.* Cambridge: Belknap Press.

Focusing on the often contentious debates over the intersection of racial and regional identities, Brundage argues that "the past" is a narrative construction that reveals power structures rather than historical fact.

Cobb, J.C. (2007). *Away Down South: A History of Southern Identity.* Oxford: Oxford University Press.

Cobb offers a critical history of the myth of Southern separateness – a region imagined to exist apart from the rest of America. He does so by discussing the interests present in various narratives about the South: the Cavalier, the "Lost Cause," and the New South, to name a few. Thus "Southern identity," taken here as an example of any identity that one might study, is not a fixed point with a linear progression but a product of the narratives told about it.

Coontz, S. (1993). *The Way We Never Were: American Families and the Nostalgia Trap.* New York: Basic Books.

The author lays bare a number of prevailing myths about the American family. She uses a wide variety of images from popular culture as well as common tropes about race, gender, and parenthood to demonstrate how the "traditional family" is actually a relatively new phenomenon of the twentieth century.

Elliott, M.A. (2007). *Custerology: The Enduring Legacy of the Indian Wars and George Armstrong Custer.* Chicago, IL: University of Chicago Press. http://dx.doi.org/10.7208/chicago/9780226201481.001.0001.

Elliot argues that all representations of history are inescapably contested and unavoidably political since they often have as much or more to do with present conditions than any attempt to recall the past. Examining how Americans and Native Americans remember the Battle of Little Bighorn, Elliot demonstrates that attempts to recall the past are always engaged in a process of choosing which community's "original" narrative is authoritative.

Flood, C. (2013). *Political Myth*. New York: Routledge.

This book offers one of the few sophisticated applications of Joseph Campbell's theory of the monomyth to distinguish how mythopoetic narratives operate in twentieth-century politics. Chapter 8 in particular provides an intriguing case study of a speech given by Charles de Gaulle in 1946 that uses nostalgia to reconstruct a heroic image of the French resistance during World War II.

Foucault, M. (1990). *The History of Sexuality: An Introduction* (Vol. 1). New York: Vintage Books.

Whether cited or not, the work of the late French scholar, Michel Foucault, informs much of our book's approach. There is so much of his work (let alone the secondary material on him) to read that newcomers may be rightly puzzled as to where they should start. This volume, though slim, is a useful introduction to his overall exercise of studying not an object but the assumptions, behaviors, and institutions which make it possible to conceive of something *as* an object about which we can think and speak, whether we like or despise it, value or ignore it. So while hardly representative of all his work, *The History of Sexuality* Vol. 1 (part of a larger set of works) offers first-time readers a chance to think over how it is that we seem to know that a distinct domain of human action is "sex," whether to be celebrated and practiced or, perhaps, hidden and denied.

Foucault, M. (2007). *Security, Territory, Population: Lectures at the Collège de France, 1977–1978*. Ed. A. Davidson. New York: Picador Press. http://dx.doi. org/10.1057/9780230245075.

This relatively late contribution within the general body of Foucault's work endeavors to resolve a central issue regarding changing forms of power in the modern world: the conceptual and practical shift away from overt exercises of sovereign authority over a particular territory toward the subtle, quotidian regulation of a particular population. Transforming the nature and influence of sovereign state power in the modern world, authorities no longer attempt to exercise absolute brute power over broad constituent populations, but rather operate so as to acutely affect them within their specific milieu. These lectures are incredibly insightful with respect to the origins of modern state governmentality and its relation to the self.

Gable, E. and R. Handler (1993). "Messing up the Past at Colonial Williamsburg," *Social Analysis: The International Journal of Social and Cultural Practice* 34, 3–16.

Using colonial Williamsburg as a case study, Gable and Handler discuss the ways in which a seemingly stable "past" becomes commodified. They delve into what kinds of things are at work in people's apparent wish to return to the "authentic" historical site and how such authenticity is manufactured to satisfy nostalgic consumers.

Habermas, J. (1991). *The Structural Transformation of the Public Sphere: An Inquiry into a Category of Bourgeois Society*. Cambridge: MIT Press.

Locating its conceptual roots in eighteenth-century western European society, Jürgen Habermas examines the emergence of the "public sphere" and proliferation of democratized speech within the modern era. Coming together across mutual concerns and common issues to form a distinct socio-political body, bourgeois private citizens constructed a collective public identity through such channels as print media, important community locales, and other democratized public resources. While many trenchant critiques have been made concerning issues of cultural and economic privilege within Habermas's reasoning, this work remains a critically important text within general studies of political systems, capitalistic organization, and the public and private realms of social life in the modern West.

Hammer, M. Gail (2011). *Imaging Religion in Film: The Politics of Nostalgia.* New York: Palgrave-Macmillan.

The author examines the intersection of religion and film, with special attention to how nostalgia in film wields social power and enables the formation of particular kinds of subjectivities.

Hoelscher, S. (2006). "The White-Pillared Past: Landscapes of Memory and Race in the American South," in R. Schein, ed., *Landscape and Race in the United States,* 39–72. New York: Routledge.

With the heritage tours of Natchez, Mississippi as his starting point, Hoelscher argues that "the past" has no fixed reference point but instead reveals the perspective of the person or group identifying it. He discusses the functions and controversies surrounding antebellum landscapes and architecture in contemporary society.

Jäger, S. (2001). "Discourse and Knowledge. Theoretical and Methodological Aspects of a Critical Discourse and Dispositive Analysis," in R. Wodak and M. Meyer, eds., *Methods of Critical Discourse Analysis,* 32–62. London: Sage. http://dx.doi.org/10.4135/9780857028020.d5.

This essay is not about origins. Instead, it is a useful guide for how to carry out critical discourse analysis based on the theoretical insights of Michel Foucault. Jäger offers very helpful instruments and instructions which can also be used for the analysis of discourses on origins.

Lincoln, B. (1994). *Authority: Construction and Corrosion.* Chicago: University of Chicago Press.

This volume studies how authority works, at a variety of cross-cultural sites, ensuring that the reader understands that what we call authority is a collaborative creation, a social product, and not a possession of any one agent.

Lincoln, B. (1996). "Mythic Narrative and Cultural Diversity in American Society," in L.L. Patton and W. Doniger, eds., *Myth and Method,* 163–76. Charlottesville, London: University of Press of Virginia.

An analysis of the movie *Avalon* (noted above) that nicely draws attention to the manner in which origins tales function to provide the impression of uniformity in social situations where, given different circumstances, fragmentation may result.

Lincoln, B. (1999). *Theorizing Myth: Narrative, Ideology, and Scholarship.* Chicago: University of Chicago Press.

Lincoln traces the history of theories regarding myth and mythmaking in the academic study of religion and points to the ideological dangers prevalent in the search for primordial origins, a search which, not surprisingly, often leads to a definitive narrative validating the researcher's theories. In short, scholarship, under particular conditions, can be little more than ideology in narrative form.

Lincoln, B. (2012). *Gods and Demons, Priests and Scholars: Critical Explorations in the History of Religions.* Chicago: University of Chicago Press.

In these essays, Lincoln repeatedly argues for a more rigorous, probing scholarship in the academic study of religion. Particularly useful for addressing the discourse of origins are the essays "Theses on Method" and "The (Un)discipline of Religious Studies."

Masuzawa, T. (1993). *In Search of Dreamtime: The Question for the Origin of Religion.* Chicago: University of Chicago Press.

Masuzawa addresses the ways in which the concept of origins has affected the discipline of religious studies, be it through the academic obsession with beginnings (in which "primitive" religion was posited as the purest form of religion), the complex relationship between originals, derivatives, and reproductions (especially in regard to the elevation of originality and authenticity in an age of rapid and cheap reproduction), or even the challenges of postmodern thinkers made upon the privileged status origination has occupied in the academy in the first place.

Masuzawa, T. (2005). *The Invention of World Religions, Or How European Universalism Was Preserved in the Language of Pluralism.* Chicago: University of Chicago Press. http://dx.doi.org/10.7208/chicago/9780226922621.001.0001.

Masuzawa's work discusses the European origins of the study and classification of various elements of culture as "the world religions" in the nineteenth century. The scholar's role in the creation and maintenance of these categories – and the implications of dividing the world in just this way – is worth considering.

Masuzawa, T. (2000). "Origin," in Willi Braun and Russell McCutcheon, eds., *Guide to the Study of Religion*, 209–24. London: Continuum.

This short chapter on the topic of the discourse on origins examines some of the assumptions underpinning certain academic quests for origins and highlights a few alternative methodologies that modern scholars might use to challenge these assumptions.

McCutcheon, Russell (2005). *Religion and Domestication of Dissent: Or, How to Live in a Less than Perfect Nation.* London, Oakville: Equinox.

Written in the wake of responses to the 9/11 attacks, in which claims concerning the original and pure Islam were routinely juxtaposed (by scholars, politicians, and journalists) with the so-called radical or extremist Islam of the attackers, this little book examines the politics and social effects of discourse on origins, purity, and authenticity, drawing on a wide variety of examples.

McPherson, T. (2003). *Reconstructing Dixie: Race, Gender, and Nostalgia in the Imagined South.* Durham: Duke University Press. http://dx.doi.org/10.1215/9780822384625.

McPherson examines ideas about the South – particularly the archetypes of the Southern lady and Southern hospitality – as discursive narratives that resonate within American culture and examines their roles in the profitable nostalgia industry.

Potter, A. (2011). *The Authenticity Hoax: Why the "Real" Things We Seek Don't Make Us Happy*. New York: Harper Perennial.

Taking up a few examples in popular culture, Potter discusses the inevitable problematics imbedded with the marketing and consumption of all things "authentic." As discourses on origins are so often intertwined with ideas about historical authenticity, his critique is a constructive one for multiple arenas.

Powers, J. (2004). *History as Propaganda: Tibetan Exiles versus the People's Republic of China*. Oxford: Oxford University Press. http://dx.doi.org/10.109 3/0195174267.001.0001.

Through an examination of histories of Tibet variously produced by the Chinese government, Tibetan authors, and western scholars, this book demonstrates that these histories offer competing origins stories designed to legitimate either Tibetan or Chinese sovereignty over the territory.

Slauter, E. (2011). *The State as a Work of Art: The Cultural Origins of the Constitution*. Chicago: University of Chicago Press.

Slauter considers the difficulty of an "original" interpretation of the United States Constitution by documenting the contested meanings of the words, ideas, and concepts used during the Constitutional era. The book tracks how group identity is bound up within these particular definitions, and demonstrates that the attempt to appeal to Constitutional origins resurrects specific political positions, rendering them natural and neutral.

Smith, J.Z. (1990). *Drudgery Divine: On the Comparison of Early Christianities and the Religions of Late Antiquity*. Chicago: University of Chicago Press.

Smith's book, focusing on how scholars study the relationship (or lack of) between earliest Christianity and other social movements from that time, provides a good discussion on how modern scholarship can become implicated in pursuing such unacademic quests for origins, and how to avoid such temptations.

White, H. (2002). "The Historical Text as Literary Artifact," in B. Richardson, ed., *Narrative Dynamics: Essays on Time, Plot, Closure, and Frames*, 191–210. Columbus, OH: Ohio State University Press.

Blurring the boundaries between historiography and literature, White argues that we should not view "history" as a neutral or innocent rendering of objective facts about the past but, rather, as its own literary invention that employs the historian's imagination and narrative conventions.

White, H. (1980). "The Value of Narrativity in the Representation of Reality," *Critical Inquiry* 7(1), 5–27. http://dx.doi.org/10.1086/448086.

White offers the genre of historiography as a way to consider narrative, discourse, and the politics at work in telling stories of – or narrativizing – events that have now come to be known as the past.

Zinn, H. (2003 [1980]). *A People's History of the United States: 1492–Present.* New York: HarperCollins.

Zinn's book offers a counter-narrative that radically shifted the way we understood American history, the origins of the country and the trajectory of its development, as well as the production of knowledge. A clear, simple read that also contains complex ideas about the work of historians, constructing origins, and how history always reflects present interests.

Index

CPSIA information can be obtained at www.ICGtesting.com
Printed in the USA
BVOW06s0505040816

457762BV00004B/32/P